Airbnb Investment Property Mortgage Loans

How to Finance and Scale a Portfolio of Short-Term Rental Properties

By Joseph G. Correa

Licensed Mortgage Broker, Finibi Mortgage

Copyright & Legal Notice

Published by Live Stronger Faster

The information provided in this book is for educational and informational purposes only and should not be construed as financial, legal, or tax advice. Readers are encouraged to consult with licensed professionals before making any financial or real estate decisions. The author and publisher assume no responsibility for any losses or damages incurred as a result of the use or misuse of the information contained in this publication.

First Edition, 2026

Table of Contents

Foreword

The transition from owning a single short-term rental property to building a scalable Airbnb portfolio is where real wealth is created, but it is also where most investors fail. Many individuals successfully purchase their first Airbnb property using enthusiasm, basic financing knowledge, and a strong belief in the income potential of short-term rentals. However, when it comes to acquiring the second, third, fourth, and tenth property, a completely different level of strategy is required. This book is designed to bridge that gap. It is not about getting started—it is about expanding intelligently, financing strategically, and building a portfolio that produces consistent, optimized cash flow over time.

Airbnb investment property mortgage loans operate in a fundamentally different way when applied to a portfolio compared to a single property. Lenders evaluate risk differently, borrowers must structure their finances more carefully, and each additional property introduces both opportunity and complexity. The mindset must shift from "Can I qualify for one property?" to "How do I structure multiple deals in a way that compounds growth while maintaining stability?" This is the foundation of scaling, and it is the core focus of this book. One of the most important concepts you will learn is that scaling is not simply about acquiring more properties—it is about acquiring them in the right sequence, with the right financing structure, and under the right conditions. Many investors make the mistake of chasing deals without considering how each new loan impacts their ability to qualify for the next one. Debt-to-income ratios, reserve requirements, credit exposure, and lender overlays all play a role in determining whether your portfolio grows smoothly or hits a hard stop. Understanding these variables in advance allows you to design a roadmap rather than reacting to obstacles after they appear.

Financing multiple Airbnb properties requires a deep understanding of the different loan products available, particularly DSCR loans, non-QM programs, and portfolio lending strategies. Unlike traditional loans that rely heavily on personal income, many Airbnb-focused financing options prioritize the income potential of the property itself. This opens the door for rapid scaling, especially for self-employed borrowers and investors who may not qualify under conventional guidelines. However, this flexibility also comes with nuances. Lenders may impose stricter reserve requirements, higher interest rates, or limitations on the number of financed properties. Navigating these trade-offs is essential for building a sustainable portfolio. Another critical element of scaling is portfolio strategy. Not all Airbnb properties are created equal, and not all markets behave the same way. Some properties generate high nightly rates but have seasonal fluctuations, while others produce consistent occupancy with lower average daily rates. A strong portfolio balances these factors, creating stability across different economic conditions. Diversification across property types, locations, and price points can reduce risk and enhance long-term performance. This book will guide you through how to think about your portfolio as a system rather than a collection of individual assets.

Cash flow optimization is equally important. It is not enough to acquire properties—you must ensure that each one contributes positively to your overall financial picture. This involves analyzing revenue potential, managing expenses, and structuring your financing in a way that maximizes returns. Small adjustments in interest rates, loan terms, or property performance can have a significant impact when multiplied across multiple properties. Learning how to evaluate these factors at scale is what separates average investors from those who build truly profitable portfolios.

As your portfolio grows, so does the importance of systems and efficiency. Managing one Airbnb property may be manageable without much structure, but managing several requires a more professional approach. From property management and pricing strategies to maintenance and guest experience, every aspect must be streamlined to support growth. Financing plays a role here as well, as lenders often assess not only your financial profile but also your experience as an operator. Demonstrating a track record of successful management can improve your access to better loan terms and more flexible programs.

Risk management is another key theme throughout this book. While Airbnb properties offer significant income potential, they also come with unique risks, including regulatory changes, market saturation, and fluctuations in travel demand. Scaling amplifies these risks if not managed properly. By structuring your loans conservatively, maintaining adequate reserves, and selecting properties with strong fundamentals, you can protect your portfolio while still pursuing aggressive growth. The goal is not to avoid risk entirely, but to control it in a way that supports long-term success.

You will also learn how to think like a lender when building your portfolio. Understanding how underwriters evaluate your applications gives you a significant advantage. Instead of guessing whether a deal will be approved, you will be able to structure it in a way that aligns with lending guidelines from the start. This includes optimizing your credit profile, managing your liabilities, and presenting your income and assets effectively. When you approach each deal with this level of clarity, your approval rate increases and your scaling process becomes more predictable.

Another powerful concept introduced in this book is the idea of stacking financing strategies. Rather than relying on a single loan type, successful investors often combine multiple approaches to achieve their goals. For example, one property may be financed using a DSCR loan, while another uses an asset-based program, and a third leverages a portfolio lender. This flexibility allows you to continue acquiring properties even when one financing path becomes limited. Learning how to navigate and combine these options is a critical skill for advanced investors.

The psychological aspect of scaling should not be overlooked. As you move from one property to multiple properties, the financial stakes increase, and so does the pressure. Decisions become more complex, and mistakes can have a larger impact. Developing confidence, discipline, and a long-term perspective is essential. This book is designed not only to provide technical knowledge but also to help you build the mindset required to operate at a higher level. The goal is to replace uncertainty with strategy and hesitation with informed action.

Throughout this book, you will gain a step-by-step

understanding of how to scale your Airbnb portfolio using the right mortgage strategies. You will learn how to identify the best financing options for each stage of growth, how to structure your deals to maximize approval chances, and how to optimize your portfolio for both cash flow and long-term appreciation. Each concept builds on the previous one, creating a comprehensive framework that you can apply immediately.

By the end of this journey, you will no longer view Airbnb properties as isolated investments. Instead, you will see them as components of a larger financial system—one that can be engineered, optimized, and expanded over time. This shift in perspective is what transforms an investor into a true portfolio builder. It is what allows you to move beyond short-term gains and create lasting wealth through real estate.

This book represents the next level in your Airbnb investment journey. Whether you currently own one property or several, the strategies outlined here will help you scale with confidence, avoid common pitfalls, and unlock the full potential of short-term rental financing. The opportunity to build a portfolio of income-producing properties has never been more accessible, but success requires knowledge, planning, and execution. As you move forward, remember that every property you acquire is not just an investment—it is a building block in a larger strategy designed to create financial freedom and long-term success.

Chapter 1

The Foundation of Scaling Airbnb Investment Properties

Scaling an Airbnb portfolio begins with a fundamental shift in thinking. Most investors approach their first property with a deal-by-deal mindset, focusing on whether a single property will cash flow, qualify for financing, and perform well in the market. While this approach is effective for getting started, it becomes limiting when the goal is to build a portfolio of multiple income-producing properties. At the portfolio level, every decision must be evaluated not only on its individual merit but also on how it contributes to the broader strategy. The foundation of scaling lies in understanding that each property is part of a system, and that system must be designed intentionally from the very beginning.

The first principle of scaling is clarity of objective. Investors often say they want more properties, but the real question is why. Is the goal to maximize monthly cash flow, build long-term appreciation, create tax advantages, or achieve financial independence within a specific timeframe? The answer to this question influences every decision that follows, including property selection, financing structure, and growth pace. For example, an investor focused on aggressive cash flow may prioritize markets with high short-term rental demand and strong average daily rates, even if appreciation is moderate. On the other hand, an investor seeking long-term wealth may accept lower cash flow in exchange for properties located in appreciating markets. Without a clear objective, scaling becomes inconsistent and inefficient.

Once the objective is defined, the next step is understanding financing capacity. Many investors underestimate how quickly traditional financing limits can be reached. Conventional loans often cap the number of financed properties, and they rely heavily on personal income and debt-to-income ratios. This creates a bottleneck for investors attempting to scale rapidly. To overcome this limitation, it is essential to transition early into financing strategies that are designed for investors, such as DSCR loans and non-QM programs. These loan types evaluate the income potential of the property rather than the borrower's personal income, allowing for greater flexibility and scalability. However, they also introduce new requirements, such as higher reserves and stronger credit positioning, which must be planned for in advance.

Another critical component of scaling is sequencing. The order in which properties are acquired can significantly impact long-term success. For example, acquiring a high-performing property early in the process can strengthen the investor's financial profile and improve qualification for subsequent loans. Conversely, taking on a marginal deal with weak cash flow can strain resources and limit future opportunities. Strategic sequencing involves prioritizing properties that not only perform well individually but also enhance the overall portfolio. This requires a forward-looking approach, where each acquisition is evaluated in the context of future deals.

Market selection plays an equally important role in building a scalable Airbnb portfolio. Not all markets are equally suited for short-term rentals, and not all markets behave the same way over time. Some areas offer high demand and strong nightly rates but are subject to strict regulations, while others provide more stability but lower income potential. A successful portfolio often includes a mix of markets, balancing risk and reward. For example, combining a high-performing vacation destination with a stable urban market can create a more resilient portfolio. Understanding local regulations, occupancy trends, and competition is essential for making informed decisions at scale.

In addition to market selection, property type must be carefully considered. Different types of properties attract different types of guests and generate different levels of income. A luxury property in a prime location may command high nightly rates but require significant upfront investment and ongoing maintenance. A smaller, more affordable property may generate consistent occupancy but lower overall revenue. Scaling effectively involves selecting properties that align with the investor's objectives while maintaining a balance between risk and return. Diversification across property types can further enhance stability and performance.

Cash flow analysis becomes increasingly important as the portfolio grows. At the single-property level, small variations in income or expenses may not have a significant impact. However, when multiplied across multiple properties, these variations can dramatically affect overall performance. Investors must develop the ability to analyze deals with precision, taking into account factors such as average daily rate, occupancy rate, operating expenses, and financing costs. This level of analysis allows for better decision-making and helps ensure that each property contributes positively to the portfolio.

Another key aspect of scaling is reserve management. Lenders often require reserves for each property, typically expressed as a number of months of mortgage payments. As the number of properties increases, so does the total reserve requirement. This can become a limiting factor if not managed properly. Investors must plan for reserves as part of their overall strategy, ensuring that they have sufficient liquidity to support both existing properties and future acquisitions. Maintaining adequate reserves also provides a buffer against unexpected events, such as market fluctuations or temporary declines in occupancy.

Operational efficiency is also critical for scaling success. Managing multiple Airbnb properties requires systems and processes that can handle increased complexity. This includes everything from guest communication and pricing strategies to cleaning and maintenance. As the portfolio grows, many investors choose to leverage property management companies or automation tools to streamline operations. While this may reduce margins slightly, it allows for greater scalability and frees up time to focus on acquiring new properties and optimizing the portfolio.

Risk management is an underlying theme that runs through every aspect of scaling. Short-term rental markets can be volatile, and regulatory changes can occur with little notice. Investors must be prepared to adapt and mitigate risks through diversification, conservative financing, and proactive management. This includes selecting properties in areas with favorable regulations, maintaining strong financial reserves, and continuously monitoring market conditions. By managing risk effectively, investors can protect their portfolios while continuing to grow.

Finally, scaling requires discipline and consistency. It is easy to become distracted by new opportunities or to deviate from the original strategy. However, long-term success is achieved by staying focused on the objective and executing the plan consistently over time. This means carefully evaluating each deal, maintaining financial discipline, and continuously refining the strategy based on experience and market conditions. Scaling is not a one-time event but an ongoing process that requires commitment and adaptability.

Real-Life Math Example: Scaling a 5-Property Airbnb Portfolio

To understand how these principles apply in practice, consider a real-life example of an investor building a portfolio of five Airbnb properties over a three-year period. The investor begins with a clear objective: to generate $10,000 per month in net cash flow while building long-term equity. The strategy involves acquiring properties that meet specific criteria, including strong short-term rental demand, favorable financing terms, and positive cash flow after expenses.

The first property is purchased for $300,000 with a 20% down payment, resulting in a loan amount of $240,000. The monthly mortgage payment, including principal, interest, taxes, and insurance, is approximately $1,800. The property generates an average daily rate of $200 with a 70% occupancy rate, resulting in gross monthly revenue of $4,200. After accounting for operating expenses such as cleaning, utilities, management, and maintenance, totaling $1,500 per month, the net cash flow is $900 per month. This property establishes the foundation for the portfolio.

Encouraged by the performance of the first property, the investor acquires a second property with similar characteristics. However, due to increased experience and improved market selection, the second property achieves a higher average daily rate of $220 and a slightly higher occupancy rate of 72%. The purchase price is $320,000 with the same 20% down payment structure. The monthly mortgage payment is $1,920, and the gross monthly revenue is approximately $4,752. After expenses of $1,600, the net cash flow is $1,232 per month. At this stage, the total portfolio cash flow is $2,132 per month.

The third property is acquired using a DSCR loan, allowing the investor to qualify based on the property's income rather than personal income. The purchase price is $350,000 with a 25% down payment, resulting in a loan amount of $262,500. The monthly mortgage payment is $2,100. This property is located in a high-demand vacation market, with an average daily rate of $250 and a 68% occupancy rate, generating gross monthly revenue of $5,100. Operating expenses are higher at $1,800 due to increased management and maintenance costs, resulting in net cash flow of $1,200 per month. The total portfolio cash flow now reaches $3,332 per month. The fourth property is strategically selected to balance the portfolio by providing more stable, year-round occupancy. The purchase price is $280,000 with a 20% down payment, and the monthly mortgage payment is $1,700. The property generates an average daily rate of $180 with a 75% occupancy rate, resulting in gross monthly revenue of $4,050. After expenses of $1,400, the net cash flow is $950 per month. The total portfolio cash flow increases to $4,282 per month.

The fifth property is a higher-end investment designed to boost overall cash flow. The purchase price is $400,000 with a 25% down payment, and the monthly mortgage payment is $2,500. The property achieves an average daily rate of $300 with a 65% occupancy rate, generating gross monthly revenue of $5,850. Operating expenses are $2,000, resulting in net cash flow of $1,350 per month. With this addition, the total portfolio cash flow reaches $5,632 per month.

Although the investor has not yet reached the initial goal of $10,000 per month, the portfolio demonstrates strong growth and scalability. Over time, increases in average daily rates, improved occupancy, and refinancing opportunities can further enhance cash flow. Additionally, the portfolio benefits from equity appreciation, which can be leveraged to acquire additional properties or optimize existing financing. This example illustrates how strategic planning, disciplined execution, and careful analysis can lead to a scalable and profitable Airbnb portfolio. By understanding the numbers behind each deal and how they contribute to the overall system, investors can make informed decisions and build a portfolio that aligns with their financial goals.

Chapter 2

Financing Strategies for Scaling Multiple Airbnb Properties

As an investor moves beyond the first few Airbnb properties, financing becomes the most critical factor determining how fast and how far a portfolio can grow. At the early stages, many investors rely on conventional loans, leveraging their personal income, credit profile, and debt-to-income ratios to qualify. While this approach can be effective for acquiring one or two properties, it quickly becomes restrictive when scaling. The transition from a beginner investor to a portfolio builder requires a deeper understanding of alternative financing strategies that are specifically designed for real estate investors, particularly those focused on short-term rentals.

The foundation of scaling financing lies in recognizing the limitations of traditional lending. Conventional loans typically impose caps on the number of financed properties, often limiting borrowers to ten or fewer. Additionally, these loans rely heavily on personal income, making it difficult for self-employed investors or those with variable income streams to qualify. As more properties are added, the borrower's debt-to-income ratio increases, eventually reaching a point where additional approvals become unlikely. This creates a bottleneck that can halt growth if alternative strategies are not implemented early.

To overcome these limitations, investors must shift toward DSCR (Debt Service Coverage Ratio) loans, which evaluate the income potential of the property rather than the borrower's personal income. This shift is a game-changer for Airbnb investors. Instead of proving income through tax returns or employment verification, the focus moves to whether the property itself generates enough revenue to cover the mortgage payment. This allows investors to scale more rapidly, especially when acquiring properties in strong short-term rental markets. However, DSCR loans come with their own considerations, including higher interest rates, larger down payment requirements, and stricter reserve expectations.

Understanding how lenders calculate DSCR is essential for optimizing financing. At its core, DSCR is the ratio of a property's income to its debt obligations. A DSCR above 1.0 indicates that the property generates enough income to cover its expenses, while a higher ratio provides a greater margin of safety. For Airbnb properties, this calculation may be based on projected short-term rental income, long-term rental estimates, or a combination of both, depending on the lender. Investors who understand how to present their property's income potential effectively can improve their chances of approval and secure better loan terms.

Another key financing strategy for scaling is the use of non-QM (non-qualified mortgage) programs. These loans are designed for borrowers who do not fit traditional underwriting guidelines, such as self-employed individuals or those with complex financial profiles. Non-QM loans may include bank statement programs, asset-based lending, and interest-only options, each offering unique advantages for investors. For example, a bank statement loan allows borrowers to qualify based on deposits rather than taxable income, which can be beneficial for those who write off significant expenses. Asset-based loans, on the other hand, focus on the borrower's liquid assets rather than income, providing another pathway for qualification.

Portfolio lenders also play a crucial role in scaling Airbnb investments. Unlike traditional lenders that sell loans on the secondary market, portfolio lenders keep loans on their own balance sheets. This gives them greater flexibility in underwriting and allows them to tailor loan terms to the specific needs of the investor. Portfolio lenders may offer customized solutions, such as blanket loans that cover multiple properties under a single mortgage, or cross-collateralization strategies that leverage equity across the portfolio. These options can simplify financing and reduce administrative complexity, making it easier to manage multiple properties.

As investors scale, managing leverage becomes increasingly important. Leverage allows investors to control more assets with less capital, but it also introduces risk. High leverage can amplify returns when properties perform well, but it can also magnify losses during downturns. Successful investors strike a balance between growth and stability, ensuring that their financing structure supports long-term sustainability. This includes maintaining sufficient reserves, avoiding overextension, and selecting loan terms that align with their cash flow objectives.

Interest rate strategy is another critical consideration in scaling financing. Higher interest rates can reduce cash flow and impact overall portfolio performance, particularly when multiple properties are involved. Investors must evaluate whether to prioritize lower rates, longer terms, or more flexible loan structures. In some cases, accepting a slightly higher rate in exchange for easier qualification or faster closing may be beneficial, especially when acquiring high-performing properties. The key is to analyze how each financing decision affects the overall portfolio rather than focusing solely on individual deals. Refinancing and equity extraction are also essential tools for scaling. As properties appreciate and equity builds, investors can access this equity through cash-out refinances or home equity lines of credit. This capital can then be reinvested into additional properties, accelerating growth. This strategy, often referred to as "equity recycling," allows investors to expand their portfolios without relying solely on new capital. However, it must be executed carefully to avoid overleveraging and to ensure that each new investment contributes positively to the portfolio.

Another important aspect of financing multiple Airbnb properties is lender diversification. Relying on a single lender can limit flexibility and increase risk if that lender changes its guidelines or reduces exposure to short-term rental properties. By working with multiple lenders, investors can access a wider range of loan products and maintain greater control over their financing strategy. This approach also allows investors to compare terms and select the best options for each deal.

Finally, scaling financing requires organization and preparation. As the number of properties increases, so does the complexity of managing loans, documentation, and financial records. Investors must maintain accurate and up-to-date records, including income statements, expense reports, and property performance data. This not only facilitates smoother loan applications but also provides valuable insights into the health of the portfolio. Being organized and proactive can significantly improve efficiency and reduce stress as the portfolio grows.

Real-Life Math Example: Financing and Scaling a Portfolio Using DSCR and Equity

Consider an investor who begins with a goal of acquiring six Airbnb properties within four years, using a combination of DSCR loans and equity extraction. The first property is purchased for $300,000 with a 20% down payment, resulting in a loan amount of $240,000. The interest rate is 7%, and the monthly mortgage payment is approximately $1,900. The property generates $4,200 in monthly revenue, with expenses of $1,500, resulting in net cash flow of $800 per month.

After one year, the property appreciates to $330,000, creating $30,000 in additional equity. The investor performs a cash-out refinance at 75% loan-to-value, resulting in a new loan amount of $247,500. After paying off the original loan, the investor receives approximately $7,500 in cash, which is combined with savings to fund the down payment for the second property.

The second property is purchased for $320,000 using a DSCR loan with a 25% down payment. The loan amount is $240,000, with a monthly payment of $2,000. The property generates $4,800 in monthly revenue and has expenses of

$1,600, resulting in net cash flow of $1,200 per month. The combined cash flow from both properties is now $2,000 per month. In the second year, both properties appreciate by 8%, increasing their combined value to approximately $702,000. The investor uses a portfolio lender to perform a blanket refinance, consolidating both loans and extracting additional equity. This results in $40,000 in available capital, which is used to acquire the third property.

The third property is purchased for $350,000 with a DSCR loan and a 25% down payment. The monthly mortgage payment is $2,200, and the property generates $5,200 in revenue with $1,800 in expenses, resulting in net cash flow of $1,200 per month. The total portfolio cash flow now reaches $3,200 per month.

By the third year, the investor repeats the process, leveraging appreciation and cash flow to acquire two additional properties. The fourth property is purchased for $280,000, generating $900 in monthly cash flow, and the fifth property is purchased for $400,000, generating $1,400 in monthly cash flow. The total portfolio cash flow increases to $5,500 per month.

In the fourth year, the investor acquires a sixth property using accumulated cash flow and equity, adding an additional

$1,500 in monthly cash flow. At this point, the portfolio consists of six properties generating a total of $7,000 per month in net cash flow. Additionally, the combined property value has grown significantly due to appreciation, creating substantial equity.

This example demonstrates how strategic financing, combined with disciplined execution, can enable rapid portfolio growth. By leveraging DSCR loans, refinancing opportunities, and equity extraction, the investor is able to scale efficiently while maintaining positive cash flow. Each step builds on the previous one, creating a compounding effect that accelerates wealth creation over time.

The key takeaway is that financing is not just a tool for acquiring properties—it is a strategy for building a scalable and sustainable portfolio. By understanding and applying these principles, investors can unlock new opportunities and achieve their long-term goals.

Chapter 3

Portfolio Strategy and Market Selection for Airbnb Scaling

As an investor transitions from acquiring individual Airbnb properties to building a scalable portfolio, the importance of portfolio strategy and market selection becomes increasingly critical. While financing provides the fuel for growth, strategy determines the direction and sustainability of that growth. Without a well-defined portfolio strategy, even the most aggressive acquisition plan can lead to instability, inconsistent cash flow, and increased risk. This chapter focuses on how to design a portfolio that is not only profitable but also resilient, scalable, and aligned with long-term financial goals.

The first concept to understand is that a portfolio is not simply a collection of properties—it is a system. Each property plays a role within that system, contributing to overall performance, risk management, and growth potential. When properties are selected without a cohesive strategy, the portfolio can become unbalanced, with some assets underperforming while others carry the financial burden. A well-structured portfolio, on the other hand, is intentionally designed to balance income, appreciation, and stability across multiple assets. Market selection is one of the most important decisions in building an

Airbnb portfolio. Different markets offer different opportunities and risks, and understanding these dynamics is essential for making informed investment decisions. High-demand vacation destinations, such as beach towns or tourist hotspots, often provide strong nightly rates and high revenue potential. However, these markets can also be highly seasonal and subject to regulatory changes. Urban markets may offer more consistent occupancy but lower average daily rates. Suburban or emerging markets can provide a balance of affordability and growth potential, making them attractive for long-term scaling.

A key strategy for portfolio success is diversification across markets. Rather than concentrating all investments in a single location, investors can spread their properties across multiple markets to reduce risk. For example, combining a high-performing vacation rental in a tourist destination with a steady, year-round rental in a suburban area can create a more stable income stream. If one market experiences a downturn due to seasonality or regulatory changes, the other properties can help offset the impact. This approach enhances resilience and reduces dependence on any single market.

Another critical factor in market selection is regulatory environment. Short-term rental regulations vary significantly from one location to another, and these rules can change over time. Some cities impose strict restrictions on Airbnb properties, including licensing requirements, occupancy limits, and zoning regulations. Others are more investor-friendly, allowing for greater flexibility and scalability. Before acquiring a property, it is essential to research local regulations and assess the long-term viability of short-term rentals in that area. Investing in markets with stable and supportive regulatory environments can reduce risk and provide greater confidence in scaling.

Property type selection is closely tied to market strategy. Different property types attract different guest demographics and generate varying levels of income. For example, a luxury property in a prime location may appeal to high-end travelers and generate significant revenue, but it also requires a larger investment and higher operating costs. A smaller, more affordable property may attract budget-conscious travelers and provide consistent occupancy, but with lower overall revenue. A balanced portfolio often includes a mix of property types, allowing investors to capture different segments of the market and optimize overall performance.

Understanding demand drivers is another essential component of market selection. Factors such as tourism trends, local attractions, business activity, and seasonal events can significantly influence short-term rental performance.

Properties located near popular attractions, beaches, or business districts often experience higher demand and occupancy rates. Additionally, markets with diverse demand drivers, such as both tourism and business travel, tend to be more stable and less susceptible to fluctuations. Analyzing these factors helps investors identify markets with strong and sustainable demand.

Cash flow optimization at the portfolio level requires a holistic approach. While individual properties may perform well, the overall portfolio must be evaluated as a whole. This includes analyzing total revenue, expenses, and financing costs across all properties. Investors should aim to create a portfolio where strong-performing properties can support those with lower performance during certain periods. This approach ensures consistent cash flow and reduces the impact of temporary fluctuations in individual property performance.

Another important aspect of portfolio strategy is scalability. Some markets and property types are easier to replicate than others. For example, if an investor finds success with a particular type of property in a specific market, they may be able to replicate that model across multiple properties. This creates efficiency in both acquisition and management, as the investor can leverage existing knowledge and systems. Identifying scalable opportunities allows for faster growth and more predictable outcomes.

Operational considerations also play a significant role in portfolio strategy. Managing properties across multiple markets requires coordination and efficient systems. Investors must decide whether to self-manage or use property management companies, and how to maintain consistent standards across all properties. Technology, such as automated pricing tools and communication platforms, can help streamline operations and improve efficiency. As the portfolio grows, operational excellence becomes a key factor in maintaining profitability and guest satisfaction.

Risk management is deeply integrated into portfolio strategy. Diversification, conservative financing, and careful market selection all contribute to reducing risk. Additionally, maintaining adequate reserves and monitoring market conditions are essential for protecting the portfolio. Investors must be prepared to adapt their strategy in response to changes in the market, whether due to economic conditions, regulatory shifts, or evolving travel trends. A proactive approach to risk management ensures long-term stability and success.

Finally, long-term vision is the guiding force behind portfolio strategy. Scaling an Airbnb portfolio is not just about acquiring properties—it is about building a system that generates sustainable income and creates lasting wealth. This requires patience, discipline, and a commitment to continuous improvement. By aligning each decision with a clear long-term vision, investors can build a portfolio that not only meets their financial goals but also provides flexibility and security for the future.

Real-Life Math Example: Building a Diversified Airbnb Portfolio Across Three Markets

To illustrate how portfolio strategy and market selection work in practice, consider an investor who builds a diversified Airbnb portfolio across three different markets over a four-year period. The investor's goal is to create a balanced portfolio that generates consistent cash flow while minimizing risk through diversification.

The first property is located in a high-demand vacation market and is purchased for $350,000. The property generates an average daily rate of $250 with a 70% occupancy rate, resulting in gross monthly revenue of approximately $5,250. Operating expenses, including cleaning, utilities, and management, total $1,800 per month. The mortgage payment is $2,200, resulting in net cash flow of $1,250 per month.

The second property is located in an urban market with more consistent demand. It is purchased for $300,000 and generates an average daily rate of $180 with a 75% occupancy rate, resulting in gross monthly revenue of $4,050. Operating expenses are $1,500, and the mortgage payment is $1,900, resulting in net cash flow of $650 per month. At this stage, the total portfolio cash flow is $1,900 per month.

The third property is located in a suburban market with strong long-term growth potential. It is purchased for $280,000 and generates an average daily rate of $160 with an 80% occupancy rate, resulting in gross monthly revenue of $3,840. Operating expenses are $1,300, and the mortgage payment is $1,700, resulting in net cash flow of $840 per month. The total portfolio cash flow increases to $2,740 per month.

In the second year, the investor adds a fourth property in the vacation market, leveraging their experience and systems. This property generates $1,400 in monthly cash flow, increasing the total portfolio cash flow to $4,140 per month. The investor then adds a fifth property in the urban market, generating $800 in monthly cash flow, bringing the total to $4,940 per month.

By the third year, the investor expands into a new market with strong tourism growth, acquiring a sixth property that generates $1,500 in monthly cash flow. The total portfolio cash flow reaches $6,440 per month. At this point, the portfolio is well-diversified across four markets, reducing exposure to any single market's fluctuations.

In the fourth year, the investor focuses on optimizing performance rather than aggressive expansion. By improving pricing strategies, increasing occupancy rates, and reducing expenses, the investor increases the average cash flow per property by $200 per month. With six properties, this results in an additional $1,200 in monthly cash flow, bringing the total to $7,640 per month.

This example demonstrates how diversification and strategic market selection can enhance both stability and profitability. By spreading investments across multiple markets and property types, the investor reduces risk while maintaining strong cash flow. Each property contributes to the overall system, creating a portfolio that is greater than the sum of its parts.

The key takeaway is that successful scaling requires more than just acquiring properties—it requires a thoughtful and intentional approach to portfolio design. By understanding market dynamics, diversifying strategically, and continuously optimizing performance, investors can build a portfolio that delivers consistent results and supports long-term financial success.

Chapter 4

Cash Flow Optimization and Performance Maximization

As an Airbnb investor transitions from acquiring properties to managing a growing portfolio, the focus must shift toward optimizing cash flow and maximizing performance. While acquisition is the engine of growth, optimization is what transforms a portfolio into a high-performing financial system. Many investors underestimate how much impact small improvements in pricing, occupancy, expenses, and financing can have when multiplied across multiple properties. This chapter explores how to fine-tune every component of your Airbnb portfolio to increase profitability, stability, and long-term scalability.

The foundation of cash flow optimization begins with understanding the core drivers of Airbnb income: average daily rate (ADR), occupancy rate, and revenue per available night. These three variables determine how much income a property can generate, and even small adjustments can significantly affect overall performance. For example, increasing the average daily rate by just $10 per night can result in hundreds or even thousands of dollars in additional annual revenue per property. When applied across a portfolio of multiple properties, the impact becomes exponential. Investors must continuously analyze and adjust these variables to remain competitive and maximize income.

Dynamic pricing is one of the most powerful tools for optimizing revenue. Unlike traditional long-term rentals, Airbnb properties operate in a constantly changing market where demand fluctuates based on seasonality, local events, and broader travel trends. Static pricing leaves money on the table during high-demand periods and reduces competitiveness during slower periods. By using dynamic pricing strategies—either manually or through automated tools—investors can adjust rates in real time to capture maximum revenue. This approach ensures that properties are priced optimally for both occupancy and profitability.

Occupancy optimization is equally important. A high average daily rate is meaningless if the property sits vacant for extended periods. Investors must strike a balance between pricing and occupancy, ensuring that properties remain attractive to guests while maintaining strong revenue. This involves analyzing booking patterns, adjusting minimum stay requirements, and offering incentives for longer stays during slower periods. Additionally, improving listing quality, including professional photography, compelling descriptions, and positive reviews, can significantly increase booking rates.

Expense management is another critical component of cash flow optimization. While revenue often receives the most attention, controlling expenses can have an equally significant impact on profitability. Common expenses include cleaning, utilities, maintenance, property management, and platform fees. Investors should regularly review these costs and identify opportunities for efficiency. For example, negotiating better rates with cleaning services, implementing energy-efficient solutions, or optimizing maintenance schedules can reduce expenses without compromising quality. Over time, these savings accumulate and enhance overall portfolio performance.

Financing structure also plays a key role in cash flow optimization. Interest rates, loan terms, and payment structures directly affect monthly cash flow. Investors should evaluate whether refinancing existing loans, extending loan terms, or adjusting interest rates can improve performance. For example, switching from a 20-year loan to a 30-year loan may reduce monthly payments and increase cash flow, even if it results in higher total interest over time. The goal is to align financing with cash flow objectives, ensuring that each property contributes positively to the portfolio.

Another important factor in performance maximization is guest experience. High-quality guest experiences lead to positive reviews, repeat bookings, and increased demand. This, in turn, allows investors to charge higher rates and maintain strong occupancy. Elements such as cleanliness, communication, amenities, and overall presentation all contribute to guest satisfaction. Investing in these areas can yield significant returns by enhancing the property's reputation and competitiveness in the market.

Portfolio-level optimization requires a broader perspective. Rather than focusing solely on individual properties, investors must evaluate how each property contributes to the overall portfolio. Some properties may generate higher cash flow, while others may provide stability or appreciation potential. By analyzing performance at the portfolio level, investors can identify opportunities to rebalance or optimize their assets. For example, underperforming properties may be improved through renovations or operational changes, while high-performing properties may justify additional investment.

Seasonality is another key consideration in Airbnb performance. Many markets experience fluctuations in demand throughout the year, with peak seasons generating significantly higher revenue. Investors must plan for these variations by setting aside reserves during high-income periods to cover potential shortfalls during slower months. Additionally, adjusting pricing and marketing strategies to align with seasonal trends can help maintain consistent performance throughout the year.

Technology and automation play an increasingly important role in optimizing Airbnb operations. Tools for dynamic pricing, automated messaging, and performance analytics can streamline processes and provide valuable insights. These tools allow investors to make data-driven decisions and respond quickly to changes in the market. As the portfolio grows, leveraging technology becomes essential for maintaining efficiency and scalability.

Risk management is closely tied to cash flow optimization. Unexpected events, such as maintenance issues, regulatory changes, or shifts in demand, can impact performance. By maintaining adequate reserves, diversifying across markets, and implementing proactive management strategies, investors can mitigate these risks and protect their cash flow. The goal is to create a portfolio that is resilient and capable of weathering fluctuations without significant disruption.

Finally, continuous improvement is the key to long-term success. The Airbnb market is dynamic, and strategies that work today may need to be adjusted in the future. Investors must remain adaptable, regularly reviewing performance and identifying opportunities for improvement. This includes staying informed about market trends, experimenting with new strategies, and learning from both successes and challenges. By committing to continuous optimization, investors can maximize the potential of their portfolio and achieve sustainable growth.

Real-Life Math Example: Increasing Cash Flow Across a 5-Property Portfolio

To demonstrate how cash flow optimization works in practice, consider an investor with a portfolio of five Airbnb properties. Each property has similar characteristics, with an average daily rate of $200 and an occupancy rate of 70%. This results in approximately 21 booked nights per month, generating $4,200 in monthly revenue per property. Operating expenses average $1,500 per month, and mortgage payments are $1,800 per month, resulting in net cash flow of $900 per property. The total portfolio cash flow is $4,500 per month.

The investor begins by implementing dynamic pricing, increasing the average daily rate by $15 during high-demand periods and adjusting pricing during slower periods. This results in an overall increase in the average daily rate to $215. With the same occupancy rate, monthly revenue per property increases to $4,515. After expenses and mortgage payments, net cash flow rises to $1,215 per property. The total portfolio cash flow increases to $6,075 per month. Next, the investor focuses on improving occupancy by enhancing listing quality and guest experience. This includes professional photography, improved descriptions, and faster response times. As a result, occupancy increases from 70% to 75%, adding approximately 1.5 additional booked nights per month. Monthly revenue per property increases to $4,837. With expenses remaining relatively stable, net cash flow rises to $1,537 per property. The total portfolio cash flow now reaches $7,685 per month.

The investor then targets expense reduction by negotiating better cleaning rates and implementing energy-efficient solutions. Monthly expenses decrease by $200 per property, resulting in expenses of $1,300 per month. This increases net cash flow to $1,737 per property. The total portfolio cash flow increases to $8,685 per month.

Finally, the investor refinances two of the properties, reducing monthly mortgage payments by $200 per property. This further increases net cash flow for those properties to $1,937 each. The remaining three properties maintain their previous cash flow levels. The total portfolio cash flow increases to approximately $9,685 per month.

Through a combination of pricing optimization, occupancy improvement, expense management, and financing adjustments, the investor has increased monthly cash flow from $4,500 to nearly $9,700. This demonstrates the power of optimization and how incremental improvements can significantly enhance portfolio performance.

The key takeaway is that cash flow optimization is not about making one large change, but rather about making multiple small improvements that compound over time. By focusing on every aspect of performance and continuously refining strategies, investors can unlock the full potential of their Airbnb portfolios and achieve their financial goals.

Chapter 5

Systems, Automation, and Scaling Operations Efficiently

As an Airbnb investor grows from managing one or two properties to operating a portfolio of multiple short-term rentals, the greatest constraint is no longer finding deals or securing financing—it is managing operations efficiently at scale. Many investors reach a point where they are overwhelmed by day-to-day tasks such as guest communication, cleaning coordination, pricing adjustments, maintenance requests, and calendar management. Without systems in place, scaling becomes chaotic, inconsistent, and ultimately unsustainable. This chapter focuses on building the operational infrastructure required to manage a growing Airbnb portfolio efficiently, profitably, and with minimal stress.

The first principle of operational scaling is recognizing that time is your most valuable asset. When managing a single property, it may be feasible to handle everything manually. However, as the number of properties increases, manual processes quickly become inefficient and error-prone. The goal is to transition from being an operator to being a systems manager. This means creating repeatable processes that can be executed consistently, either through automation or delegation. By doing so, investors can free up time to focus on higher-value activities such as acquisitions, financing, and portfolio optimization.

Standardization is the foundation of scalable operations. Each property should follow a consistent set of processes, from guest communication to cleaning protocols to maintenance procedures. Standardization ensures that every property delivers a consistent guest experience, regardless of location or size. This includes creating templates for guest messages, check-in instructions, and review requests, as well as establishing clear guidelines for cleaning and maintenance. When processes are standardized, they can be easily replicated across new properties, reducing the complexity of scaling.

Automation is a powerful tool for improving efficiency and reducing workload. Many aspects of Airbnb management can be automated, including guest communication, pricing adjustments, and booking management. Automated messaging systems can send check-in instructions, reminders, and follow-up messages without requiring manual input. Dynamic pricing tools can adjust rates in real time based on demand, ensuring optimal pricing without constant monitoring. Calendar synchronization tools can prevent double bookings and streamline scheduling across multiple platforms. By leveraging automation, investors can manage more properties with less effort. Delegation is another key component of scaling operations. While automation can handle many tasks, certain responsibilities require human involvement. This includes cleaning, maintenance, and guest support. Investors must decide whether to build an in-house team or work with third-party service providers. Each approach has its advantages and challenges. In-house teams offer greater control and consistency, while third-party providers offer flexibility and scalability. The choice depends on the investor's goals, resources, and portfolio size. Regardless of the approach, clear communication and expectations are essential for maintaining quality and efficiency.

Property management companies can also play a significant role in scaling operations. For investors who prefer a more hands-off approach, property managers can handle day-to-day operations, including guest communication, cleaning coordination, and maintenance. While this typically involves a management fee, it allows investors to focus on growth and strategy rather than operations. However, it is important to carefully evaluate property managers to ensure they align with your standards and objectives. Not all management companies are equal, and selecting the right partner can have a significant impact on performance.

Technology integration is critical for managing a growing portfolio. Property management systems (PMS) serve as the central hub for managing bookings, calendars, and guest communication. These systems can integrate with multiple booking platforms, providing a unified view of all properties. Additionally, analytics tools can provide insights into performance, allowing investors to identify trends and make data-driven decisions. As the portfolio grows, having a centralized system becomes essential for maintaining organization and efficiency.

Quality control is another important aspect of scaling operations. As processes become more automated and tasks are delegated, maintaining consistent quality becomes a challenge. Investors must implement systems for monitoring performance, such as regular property inspections, guest feedback analysis, and performance metrics. This ensures that standards are maintained across all properties and that any issues are addressed promptly. Consistent quality is essential for maintaining positive reviews and high occupancy rates.

Maintenance management becomes increasingly complex as the number of properties grows. Unexpected issues such as plumbing problems, appliance failures, or general wear and tear can disrupt operations and impact guest satisfaction. Having a reliable network of contractors and service providers is essential for addressing these issues quickly and efficiently. Preventative maintenance strategies, such as regular inspections and scheduled servicing, can also reduce the likelihood of major problems and extend the lifespan of property assets.

Communication systems must also evolve as the portfolio scales. Efficient communication between investors, property managers, cleaners, and maintenance teams is essential for smooth operations. Centralized communication platforms can help streamline this process, ensuring that all parties are informed and aligned. Clear communication reduces the risk of errors, improves response times, and enhances overall efficiency.

Another critical element of operational scaling is performance tracking. Investors must monitor key performance indicators such as occupancy rate, average daily rate, revenue, expenses, and guest satisfaction. By analyzing these metrics, investors can identify areas for improvement and make informed decisions. Performance tracking also allows investors to compare properties and identify best practices that can be applied across the portfolio.

Scalability requires flexibility and adaptability. As the portfolio grows, new challenges and opportunities will arise. Investors must be willing to adjust their systems and processes to accommodate growth and changing market conditions. This includes adopting new technologies, refining operational strategies, and continuously improving efficiency. A flexible approach ensures that the portfolio can adapt to changes and continue to grow sustainably.

Finally, mindset plays a crucial role in operational scaling. Investors must shift from a hands-on approach to a leadership role, focusing on strategy and oversight rather than day-to-day tasks. This requires trust in systems, processes, and team members. By building a strong operational foundation, investors can create a portfolio that runs efficiently and generates consistent income, allowing them to focus on long-term growth and financial freedom.

Real-Life Math Example: Scaling Operations from 2 to 8 Airbnb Properties

Consider an investor who starts with two Airbnb properties, each generating $4,500 in monthly revenue. Operating expenses, including cleaning, utilities, and maintenance, total $1,500 per property, and mortgage payments are $1,800 per property. This results in net cash flow of $1,200 per property, or $2,400 total per month. At this stage, the investor manages both properties manually, handling guest communication, pricing, and coordination with cleaners. As the investor acquires two additional properties, bringing the total to four, operational complexity increases. Without systems in place, the investor spends an additional 20 hours per week managing tasks. This limits their ability to focus on acquiring new properties. To address this, the investor implements automation tools for messaging and pricing, reducing manual workload by 50%. This allows them to maintain efficiency while managing four properties.

With improved systems, the investor expands to six properties. At this stage, they hire a part-time assistant for $1,000 per month to handle guest communication and coordination. This reduces their workload further and allows them to focus on growth. Each property continues to generate $1,200 in net cash flow, resulting in total cash flow of $7,200 per month. After accounting for the assistant's cost, net cash flow is $6,200 per month.

The investor then scales to eight properties and transitions to a more structured operation. They hire a cleaning team at negotiated rates, reducing cleaning costs by $100 per property. This results in savings of $800 per month across eight properties. Additionally, they implement a property management system costing $200 per month, which improves efficiency and reduces errors. The total operational cost increases slightly, but efficiency gains and cost savings offset these expenses. With optimized operations, each property now generates $1,300 in net cash flow due to improved efficiency and reduced expenses. Across eight properties, total cash flow reaches $10,400 per month. After accounting for operational costs, including the assistant and software, net cash flow is approximately $9,200 per month.

This example demonstrates how systems, automation, and delegation can enable efficient scaling. By reducing workload, improving efficiency, and optimizing costs, the investor is able to grow their portfolio without being overwhelmed by operations. The key takeaway is that operational scaling is not just about managing more properties—it is about managing them more effectively.

By building strong systems and leveraging automation and delegation, investors can create a scalable operation that supports long-term growth and profitability. Each improvement compounds over time, allowing the portfolio to expand while maintaining high performance and efficiency.

Chapter 6

Risk Management and Protecting Your Airbnb Portfolio

As an Airbnb investor scales from a few properties to a multi-property portfolio, risk management becomes one of the most important—and often overlooked—components of long-term success. While growth and cash flow are exciting, they also introduce increased exposure to financial, operational, and market risks. Without a structured approach to risk management, even a high-performing portfolio can quickly become vulnerable to unexpected disruptions. This chapter focuses on identifying, analyzing, and mitigating risks so that your Airbnb portfolio remains stable, resilient, and profitable over time.

The first step in effective risk management is understanding that risk is not something to be avoided entirely—it is something to be controlled. Every investment carries some level of risk, but successful investors learn how to manage that risk strategically. This begins with identifying the primary categories of risk associated with Airbnb properties, including market risk, regulatory risk, operational risk, financial risk, and property-specific risk. Each of these categories can impact your portfolio in different ways, and each requires a unique strategy for mitigation.

Market risk is one of the most significant factors affecting Airbnb performance. Short-term rental demand can fluctuate due to economic conditions, changes in travel trends, or increased competition. For example, during economic downturns, discretionary travel may decrease, leading to lower occupancy rates. Similarly, an influx of new Airbnb listings in a particular market can reduce pricing power and increase competition. To mitigate market risk, investors should diversify their portfolio across multiple markets and property types. This reduces reliance on any single location and creates a more balanced income stream.

Regulatory risk is another critical consideration. Short-term rental regulations vary widely by location and can change with little notice. Some cities impose strict limits on Airbnb operations, including licensing requirements, occupancy restrictions, and zoning laws. In extreme cases, short-term rentals may be banned altogether. Investors must stay informed about local regulations and prioritize markets with stable, investor-friendly policies. Additionally, having contingency plans—such as the ability to convert a property to a long-term rental—can provide a safety net in the event of regulatory changes. Operational risk increases as the number of properties grows. Managing multiple properties introduces complexity, and small issues can quickly escalate if not handled properly. For example, a delayed cleaning or maintenance issue can lead to negative reviews, which can impact future bookings. To mitigate operational risk, investors must implement strong systems and processes, including standardized procedures, reliable service providers, and quality control measures. Automation and delegation can also reduce the likelihood of errors and improve overall efficiency.

Financial risk is closely tied to leverage and cash flow management. While leverage allows investors to scale quickly, it also increases exposure to financial instability. High debt levels can become problematic if cash flow decreases or expenses increase unexpectedly. Investors must carefully manage their financing structure, ensuring that each property generates positive cash flow and that sufficient reserves are maintained. A conservative approach to leverage, combined with strong cash flow, provides a buffer against financial shocks.

Property-specific risk includes factors such as location, property condition, and guest-related issues. For example, properties in flood-prone areas or regions with high crime rates may face additional challenges. Similarly, poorly maintained properties can lead to higher expenses and lower guest satisfaction. Investors should conduct thorough due diligence before acquiring a property, including inspections, market analysis, and risk assessment. Additionally, maintaining proper insurance coverage is essential for protecting against unforeseen events such as property damage or liability claims.

Insurance plays a vital role in risk management. Standard homeowner's insurance policies may not fully cover short-term rental activities, so investors should ensure they have appropriate coverage for Airbnb operations. This may include specialized short-term rental insurance, liability coverage, and protection against loss of income. While insurance adds to operating costs, it provides critical protection and peace of mind.

Reserve management is another key component of risk mitigation. Maintaining adequate financial reserves allows investors to handle unexpected expenses, such as major repairs or temporary declines in occupancy. A common guideline is to maintain at least three to six months of expenses for each property. As the portfolio grows, reserve requirements increase, making it essential to plan and manage liquidity carefully. Strong reserves provide stability and reduce the risk of financial distress. Diversification is one of the most effective strategies for reducing risk. By spreading investments across different markets, property types, and price points, investors can create a more resilient portfolio. For example, combining high-end luxury properties with more affordable, high-occupancy units can balance income and risk. Similarly, investing in both seasonal and year-round markets can reduce the impact of fluctuations in demand.

Another important aspect of risk management is monitoring and adaptability. The Airbnb market is dynamic, and conditions can change rapidly. Investors must continuously monitor performance, market trends, and regulatory developments. By staying informed and adapting strategies as needed, investors can respond proactively to changes and minimize potential risks. This includes adjusting pricing, refining operations, and exploring new markets or opportunities.

Stress testing is a valuable tool for evaluating portfolio resilience. This involves analyzing how the portfolio would perform under different scenarios, such as a 20% drop in occupancy or an increase in expenses. By understanding these potential outcomes, investors can identify weaknesses and implement strategies to strengthen their portfolio. Stress testing provides insight into the level of risk and helps ensure that the portfolio can withstand adverse conditions.

Finally, mindset is a critical factor in risk management. Investors must approach scaling with a balance of ambition and caution. While growth is important, it should not come at the expense of stability. By prioritizing sustainability and long-term success, investors can build a portfolio that not only generates income but also withstands challenges and uncertainties.

Real-Life Math Example: Stress Testing and Protecting a 6-Property Portfolio

Consider an investor with a portfolio of six Airbnb properties, each generating $5,000 in monthly revenue. Operating expenses average $1,800 per property, and mortgage payments are $2,200 per property. This results in net cash flow of $1,000 per property, or $6,000 total per month. The portfolio appears strong under normal conditions, but the investor wants to evaluate its resilience under different scenarios.

First, the investor analyzes the impact of a 20% decline in occupancy due to a market downturn. Monthly revenue per property decreases from $5,000 to $4,000. Operating expenses remain relatively fixed at $1,800, and mortgage payments remain at $2,200. This results in net cash flow of $0 per property. The total portfolio cash flow drops from $6,000 to $0, highlighting the importance of maintaining reserves.

Next, the investor evaluates the impact of increased expenses. Suppose operating expenses increase by $300 per property due to higher cleaning and maintenance costs. Total expenses per property rise to $2,100, reducing net cash flow to $700 per property. The total portfolio cash flow decreases to $4,200 per month. While still positive, this reduction demonstrates how sensitive cash flow can be to expense changes.

The investor then considers a worst-case scenario where both occupancy declines and expenses increase. Revenue drops to $4,000, and expenses rise to $2,100, resulting in a net loss of $300 per property after accounting for mortgage payments. The total portfolio experiences a monthly loss of $1,800. This scenario emphasizes the importance of having financial reserves to cover temporary losses.

To mitigate these risks, the investor maintains six months of reserves for each property. With monthly expenses of $4,000 per property (including mortgage and operating costs), this requires $24,000 in reserves per property, or $144,000 for the entire portfolio. While this is a significant amount, it provides a strong safety net and ensures that the investor can weather downturns without financial distress.

The investor also diversifies the portfolio across three different markets, reducing the likelihood that all properties will be affected simultaneously by market fluctuations. Additionally, they implement dynamic pricing and operational efficiencies to improve performance and maintain competitiveness. By stress testing the portfolio and implementing risk mitigation strategies, the investor is able to identify potential vulnerabilities and strengthen their financial position. This proactive approach ensures that the portfolio remains stable and resilient, even in challenging conditions.

The key takeaway is that risk management is not about eliminating risk—it is about preparing for it. By understanding potential challenges and implementing strategies to address them, investors can protect their portfolios and continue to grow with confidence.

Chapter 7

Scaling Beyond Limits – Advanced Growth, Deal Flow, and Long-Term Wealth Strategy

As an Airbnb investor masters financing, optimization, systems, and risk management, the next phase is breaking through growth ceilings and scaling beyond what most investors believe is possible. At this level, success is no longer driven by individual deals or incremental improvements—it is driven by strategy, deal flow, leverage, and long-term vision. This chapter focuses on how to move from owning multiple properties to building a true Airbnb investment empire, where growth becomes predictable, scalable, and compounding.

One of the biggest challenges investors face at this stage is hitting a growth plateau. This often occurs when financing limits are reached, deal flow slows down, or operational complexity becomes overwhelming. To overcome this, investors must shift from a reactive approach—waiting for deals—to a proactive system that consistently generates opportunities. Deal flow becomes the lifeblood of scaling, and investors must build systems that continuously identify, analyze, and secure high-quality Airbnb investment opportunities. Creating consistent deal flow requires a multi-channel approach. Investors can leverage direct marketing, real estate agents, wholesalers, online platforms, and data tools to identify potential properties. Off-market deals often provide the best opportunities, as they involve less competition and more flexibility in pricing and terms. By building relationships with agents, wholesalers, and property owners, investors can position themselves as the go-to buyer for Airbnb properties. Over time, this network becomes a powerful asset, providing a steady stream of opportunities.

Another advanced growth strategy is leveraging partnerships. Rather than relying solely on personal capital and credit, investors can collaborate with partners to expand their capacity. This may involve joint ventures, private money investors, or equity partnerships. For example, one partner may provide capital while the other manages operations, creating a mutually beneficial arrangement. Partnerships allow investors to scale faster and take on larger deals without overextending themselves financially. However, clear agreements and alignment of goals are essential for successful partnerships.

Entity structuring becomes increasingly important as the portfolio grows. Operating under the right legal and financial structure can provide benefits such as liability protection, tax advantages, and improved financing opportunities. Many investors choose to hold properties in LLCs or other entities, separating personal and business assets. Additionally, structuring properties across multiple entities can enhance scalability and reduce risk. Working with legal and financial professionals ensures that the structure aligns with long-term goals.

Capital allocation is another critical factor in advanced scaling. Investors must decide how to deploy capital effectively, balancing acquisitions, improvements, and reserves. Not all opportunities are equal, and prioritizing high-return investments is essential for maximizing growth. This involves analyzing potential returns, risk levels, and strategic fit within the portfolio. By allocating capital efficiently, investors can accelerate growth while maintaining stability.

At this stage, investors also begin to think in terms of portfolio-level leverage rather than individual property financing. This may include cross-collateralization, blanket loans, or portfolio lines of credit. These strategies allow investors to leverage the combined value of multiple properties, unlocking additional capital for expansion. While this approach can significantly accelerate growth, it must be used carefully to avoid excessive risk. Another key concept is building a scalable acquisition model. Instead of evaluating each deal from scratch, investors can develop criteria and systems that streamline the acquisition process. This includes defining target markets, property types, price ranges, and performance metrics. By standardizing these criteria, investors can quickly identify suitable opportunities and make decisions more efficiently. This approach reduces analysis paralysis and enables faster growth.

Long-term wealth strategy is the ultimate goal of scaling. Airbnb properties provide both cash flow and appreciation, creating multiple avenues for wealth creation. Investors must decide how to balance these factors based on their objectives. Some may prioritize cash flow for immediate income, while others focus on appreciation for long-term wealth. A well-rounded strategy often includes a combination of both, providing flexibility and financial security.

Exit strategies are also an important consideration. While the focus is on scaling, investors should plan for eventual exits, whether through property sales, portfolio sales, or refinancing. Having a clear exit strategy ensures that investments align with long-term goals and provides options for realizing gains. For example, selling underperforming properties and reinvesting in higher-performing assets can improve overall portfolio performance.

Another advanced strategy is creating additional revenue streams from the Airbnb portfolio. This may include upselling services, offering experiences, or leveraging the brand to create new opportunities. For example, investors can create guides, courses, or consulting services based on their expertise. These additional income streams enhance overall profitability and diversify revenue sources.

Technology and data become even more critical at this level. Advanced analytics tools can provide insights into market trends, pricing strategies, and performance metrics. By leveraging data, investors can make informed decisions and stay ahead of the competition. This includes identifying emerging markets, optimizing pricing, and improving operational efficiency.

Scaling beyond limits also requires a strong mindset. At this level, challenges become more complex, and decisions carry greater consequences. Investors must develop confidence, resilience, and a long-term perspective. This includes embracing calculated risks, learning from mistakes, and continuously improving. The ability to think strategically and adapt to changing conditions is what separates top investors from the rest.

Finally, building an Airbnb empire is not just about financial success—it is about creating a system that supports your desired lifestyle. Whether the goal is financial independence, time freedom, or legacy building, the portfolio should align with your personal vision. By maintaining clarity of purpose and focusing on long-term goals, investors can build a portfolio that delivers both financial and personal fulfillment.

Real-Life Math Example: Scaling from 6 to 15 Airbnb Properties Using Advanced Strategies

Consider an investor who has successfully built a portfolio of six Airbnb properties, each generating $1,200 in monthly cash flow, for a total of $7,200 per month. The combined property value is $2.1 million, with an average loan-to-value ratio of 70%, resulting in $630,000 in equity. The investor's goal is to scale to 15 properties within five years while increasing monthly cash flow to over $20,000.

The investor begins by leveraging existing equity through a portfolio line of credit, accessing $200,000 in usable capital. This capital is used as down payments for three additional properties, each priced at $350,000 with 25% down payments of $87,500. These properties generate $1,300 in monthly cash flow each, adding $3,900 to the portfolio. The total portfolio now consists of nine properties generating $11,100 per month.

Next, the investor forms a partnership with a private investor who provides $300,000 in capital in exchange for a 50% share of profits on new acquisitions. Using this capital, the investor acquires four additional properties, each generating $1,400 in monthly cash flow. The investor's share of the cash flow is $700 per property, adding $2,800 to their income. The total portfolio now generates $13,900 per month.

In the following year, the investor identifies two off-market deals priced below market value at $300,000 each. By negotiating favorable terms and using a combination of equity and cash flow, the investor acquires both properties with minimal out-of-pocket expense. These properties generate $1,500 in monthly cash flow each, adding $3,000 to the portfolio. The total monthly cash flow reaches $16,900.

To reach the goal of 15 properties, the investor continues to optimize existing properties, increasing average cash flow by $200 per property through pricing and operational improvements. With 11 owned properties and 4 partnered properties, this results in an additional $3,000 in monthly cash flow. The total portfolio cash flow now exceeds $19,900 per month.

Finally, the investor acquires two additional properties using accumulated cash flow and refinancing strategies. Each property generates $1,200 in monthly cash flow, adding $2,400 to the total. The portfolio now consists of 15 properties generating over $22,000 per month in net cash flow. This example demonstrates how advanced strategies such as equity leverage, partnerships, and deal flow systems can accelerate growth beyond traditional limits. By combining multiple approaches and maintaining a strategic focus, the investor is able to achieve significant scale and financial success.

The key takeaway is that scaling beyond limits requires a shift in thinking—from individual deals to systems, from personal capacity to leveraged growth, and from short-term gains to long-term wealth. By mastering these advanced strategies, investors can build a portfolio that not only grows but thrives at scale.

Chapter 8

Refinancing, Cash-Out Strategies, and Equity Recycling for Rapid Growth

As an Airbnb investor builds a portfolio of income-producing properties, one of the most powerful tools for accelerating growth is not just acquiring new properties—but unlocking the capital already trapped inside existing ones. This capital, known as equity, represents one of the most underutilized resources in real estate investing. While many investors focus solely on saving for down payments or increasing income, advanced investors understand how to recycle equity strategically to fund additional acquisitions without significantly increasing their personal financial burden. This chapter focuses on how refinancing, cash-out strategies, and equity recycling can be used to scale an Airbnb portfolio faster and more efficiently.

Equity is created in two primary ways: through appreciation and through loan paydown. As property values increase over time and mortgage balances decrease, the gap between the property's value and the loan amount widens. This gap represents usable capital that can be accessed through refinancing or other lending products. However, equity alone does not generate cash flow—it must be converted into usable capital through strategic financing. This is where refinancing and cash-out strategies come into play.

A cash-out refinance is one of the most common methods for accessing equity. In this process, the investor replaces the existing mortgage with a new, larger loan based on the current value of the property. The difference between the new loan amount and the existing loan balance is received as cash, which can then be used for additional investments. For Airbnb investors, this strategy is particularly effective because it allows them to reinvest profits into new properties, creating a compounding effect that accelerates portfolio growth.

Timing is critical when executing a cash-out refinance. Refinancing too early may limit the amount of equity available, while waiting too long may result in missed opportunities. Investors must monitor property values, market conditions, and loan terms to determine the optimal time to refinance. Additionally, lenders typically require a seasoning period—often six to twelve months—before allowing a cash-out refinance. Understanding these timelines helps investors plan their growth strategy more effectively.

Another important consideration is loan-to-value (LTV) ratio. Most lenders limit cash-out refinances to 70–75% of the property's value for investment properties. This means that investors must leave a portion of equity in the property, which acts as a buffer for both the lender and the investor. While this may seem restrictive, it also helps maintain stability and reduces the risk of overleveraging. Investors must carefully calculate how much equity can be accessed while ensuring that the property continues to generate positive cash flow after refinancing.

Debt Service Coverage Ratio (DSCR) loans play a significant role in refinancing Airbnb properties. Because these loans are based on the property's income rather than personal income, they are well-suited for investors with multiple properties. When refinancing under a DSCR program, lenders evaluate whether the property's income can support the new loan amount. This makes it essential for investors to optimize property performance before refinancing, as higher income can lead to better loan terms and greater access to equity.

Equity recycling is the process of repeatedly accessing equity from existing properties and reinvesting it into new acquisitions. This creates a cycle of growth where each property contributes to the acquisition of the next. Over time, this compounding effect can significantly accelerate portfolio expansion. However, equity recycling must be executed carefully to avoid excessive leverage and maintain financial stability. Each new investment should be evaluated to ensure that it strengthens the overall portfolio rather than introducing unnecessary risk.

Another strategy for accessing equity is the use of home equity lines of credit (HELOCs). Unlike a cash-out refinance, which provides a lump sum of cash, a HELOC offers a revolving line of credit that can be drawn upon as needed. This provides flexibility and allows investors to access funds quickly for new opportunities. However, HELOCs typically have variable interest rates, which can introduce additional risk. Investors must weigh the benefits of flexibility against the potential for increased costs.

Portfolio-level refinancing is an advanced strategy that involves refinancing multiple properties under a single loan. This approach can simplify financing, reduce administrative complexity, and provide access to larger amounts of capital. Portfolio lenders often offer more flexible terms, allowing investors to structure loans in a way that aligns with their growth strategy. However, this approach also ties multiple properties together, which can increase risk if not managed carefully.

Cash-out strategies are not limited to refinancing. Investors can also access equity through the sale of underperforming properties. By selling a property that has appreciated in value, investors can unlock capital and reinvest it into higher-performing assets. This strategy, known as portfolio optimization, allows investors to continuously improve the quality and performance of their portfolio over time.

Interest rates and loan terms are critical factors in refinancing decisions. While accessing equity can accelerate growth, higher interest rates can reduce cash flow and impact overall performance. Investors must evaluate whether the benefits of accessing equity outweigh the costs associated with refinancing. In some cases, it may be advantageous to delay refinancing until more favorable terms are available. Strategic timing and careful analysis are essential for maximizing the benefits of refinancing.

Tax considerations also play a role in equity recycling strategies. While cash-out refinance proceeds are generally not considered taxable income, the increased debt can affect overall financial planning. Additionally, selling properties may trigger capital gains taxes, which must be factored into decision-making. Working with a tax professional can help investors optimize their strategies and minimize tax liabilities.

Risk management remains a central theme when leveraging equity. While equity recycling can accelerate growth, it also increases exposure to market fluctuations and financial instability. Investors must maintain adequate reserves, avoid overleveraging, and ensure that each property contributes positively to the portfolio. A balanced approach allows for growth while preserving stability and resilience.

Ultimately, refinancing and equity recycling are powerful tools for scaling an Airbnb portfolio. By unlocking the value of existing properties and reinvesting it strategically, investors can create a cycle of growth that compounds over time. However, success requires careful planning, disciplined execution, and a focus on long-term sustainability. When used effectively, these strategies can transform a modest portfolio into a substantial real estate empire.

Real-Life Math Example: Using Cash-Out Refinancing to Scale from 4 to 10 Properties

Consider an investor who owns four Airbnb properties, each valued at $350,000. The total portfolio value is $1.4 million, with an average loan balance of $245,000 per property, resulting in a total loan balance of $980,000. This creates $420,000 in equity across the portfolio. The investor's goal is to use this equity to acquire additional properties and scale to ten properties within three years.

The investor begins by performing a cash-out refinance on the first property. The property has appreciated to $370,000, and the lender allows a 75% loan-to-value ratio. This results in a new loan amount of $277,500. After paying off the existing loan of $245,000, the investor receives $32,500 in cash. This process is repeated for the remaining three properties, generating a total of $130,000 in available capital.

Using this capital, the investor acquires two additional properties, each priced at $300,000 with 25% down payments of $75,000. The total investment required is $150,000, which is covered by the cash-out proceeds and additional savings. Each property generates $1,200 in monthly cash flow, adding $2,400 to the portfolio.

In the following year, the investor repeats the process as the properties appreciate further. The six properties are now valued at an average of $380,000, creating additional equity. By refinancing again, the investor accesses another $150,000 in capital, which is used to acquire two more properties. These properties generate $1,300 in monthly cash flow each, adding $2,600 to the portfolio.

By the third year, the investor has eight properties generating a total of $9,000 in monthly cash flow. Through continued appreciation and optimization, the investor performs another round of refinancing, accessing $120,000 in capital. This is used to acquire two final properties, each generating $1,400 in monthly cash flow. The portfolio now consists of ten properties generating $11,800 per month.

Throughout this process, the investor carefully manages leverage, ensuring that each property maintains positive cash flow and that sufficient reserves are maintained. By strategically using cash-out refinancing and equity recycling, the investor is able to scale from four to ten properties without relying solely on new capital.

This example illustrates the power of equity as a growth tool. By unlocking and reinvesting equity, investors can accelerate their portfolio expansion and achieve their financial goals more efficiently. The key is to approach these strategies with discipline, planning, and a focus on long-term sustainability.

Chapter 9

Scaling Airbnb with Multi-Unit Properties and Mixed Rental Models

As Airbnb investors advance in their journey, one of the most powerful ways to accelerate growth and efficiency is by transitioning from single-family properties to multi-unit investments. Duplexes, triplexes, fourplexes, and small multifamily properties offer a unique opportunity to scale faster, increase income density, and optimize operations. Instead of acquiring one door at a time, investors can acquire multiple income-producing units under a single property, creating both operational and financial advantages. This chapter focuses on how to strategically use multi-unit properties and mixed rental models to scale an Airbnb portfolio more efficiently and profitably.

The concept of income density is central to multi-unit investing. With single-family homes, each property generates income from one rental unit. In contrast, a duplex generates income from two units, a triplex from three, and a fourplex from four. This means that a single acquisition can significantly increase total revenue and cash flow. Additionally, certain expenses—such as land cost, insurance, and maintenance—are shared across multiple units, improving overall efficiency. This allows investors to achieve higher returns with fewer transactions.

Financing multi-unit Airbnb properties requires a slightly different approach compared to single-family homes. Properties with two to four units are often still eligible for residential financing, including DSCR and non-QM loans. This provides flexibility and allows investors to scale without immediately transitioning into commercial lending. However, lenders may apply different underwriting standards, including stricter appraisal requirements and more detailed income analysis. Understanding these nuances is essential for successfully acquiring multi-unit properties.

One of the key advantages of multi-unit properties is the ability to implement mixed rental models. Instead of operating all units as short-term rentals, investors can combine short-term, mid-term, and long-term rental strategies within the same property. For example, one unit may be used for Airbnb guests, while another is rented to a long-term tenant, and a third is used for mid-term stays such as traveling professionals. This diversification of income streams reduces risk and provides greater stability, especially in markets with fluctuating short-term rental demand.

Mixed rental models also offer flexibility in response to regulatory changes. If local regulations restrict short-term rentals, investors can adjust their strategy by converting some units to mid-term or long-term rentals. This adaptability ensures that the property continues to generate income even under changing conditions. It also provides a safety net that single-strategy properties may lack.

Operational efficiency is another major benefit of multi-unit properties. Managing multiple units within a single property is often more efficient than managing multiple separate properties. Cleaning, maintenance, and guest communication can be streamlined, reducing both time and costs. For example, a single cleaning team can service all units in one location, and maintenance issues can be addressed more quickly due to proximity. This efficiency becomes increasingly valuable as the portfolio grows.

Market selection remains critical when investing in multi-unit Airbnb properties. Not all markets are suitable for short-term rentals, and zoning regulations can vary significantly. Investors must ensure that multi-unit properties are located in areas where short-term rentals are permitted and where demand supports multiple units. Additionally, properties in high-demand areas with strong tourism or business travel tend to perform better, as they can sustain higher occupancy rates across multiple units. Property layout and design also play a significant role in the success of multi-unit Airbnb investments. Units should be designed to maximize privacy, comfort, and functionality for guests. Separate entrances, soundproofing, and dedicated amenities can enhance the guest experience and improve reviews. Well-designed properties are more likely to achieve higher occupancy rates and command premium pricing, which directly impacts cash flow.

Cash flow analysis for multi-unit properties must account for both the benefits and the complexities of multiple units. While revenue potential is higher, expenses may also increase due to additional cleaning, utilities, and maintenance. Investors must carefully analyze each unit's performance and ensure that the overall property generates positive cash flow. This includes evaluating average daily rates, occupancy rates, and operating costs for each unit.

Another important consideration is scalability. Multi-unit properties allow investors to grow their portfolios more quickly by increasing the number of units per acquisition. This reduces the time and effort required to achieve a certain level of income. For example, acquiring a fourplex can provide the equivalent of four single-family properties in a single transaction. This efficiency is particularly valuable for investors aiming to scale rapidly. Risk management is also enhanced with multi-unit properties. If one unit experiences a vacancy or temporary decline in performance, the other units can continue to generate income, offsetting the impact. This diversification within a single property reduces overall risk and provides a more stable income stream. However, investors must still maintain reserves and implement strong management practices to mitigate potential challenges.

Financing strategies for multi-unit properties can also include creative approaches such as house hacking. In some cases, investors may occupy one unit while renting out the others, qualifying for more favorable financing terms. While this strategy is more common in the early stages of investing, it can still be a valuable tool for acquiring multi-unit properties with lower upfront costs.

Long-term wealth creation is a key advantage of multi-unit Airbnb investments. In addition to generating strong cash flow, these properties often appreciate in value over time, creating additional equity. This equity can be leveraged for future acquisitions, further accelerating portfolio growth. By combining income generation with appreciation, investors can build substantial wealth over time.

Ultimately, multi-unit properties and mixed rental models provide a powerful pathway for scaling an Airbnb portfolio. By increasing income density, improving operational efficiency, and diversifying income streams, investors can achieve faster growth and greater stability. However, success requires careful planning, market analysis, and execution. When approached strategically, multi-unit investing can transform an Airbnb portfolio into a highly efficient and profitable system.

Real-Life Math Example: Scaling with a 4-Unit Airbnb Property and Mixed Rental Strategy

Consider an investor who purchases a fourplex for $600,000 in a high-demand short-term rental market. The investor uses a DSCR loan with a 25% down payment of $150,000, resulting in a loan amount of $450,000. The monthly mortgage payment, including taxes and insurance, is approximately $3,200.

The investor decides to implement a mixed rental model. Two units are operated as short-term rentals, one unit is rented as a mid-term rental to traveling professionals, and one unit is leased as a long-term rental. This diversified approach provides both high income potential and stability.

The two Airbnb units each generate an average daily rate of $180 with a 70% occupancy rate. This results in approximately 21 booked nights per month, generating $3,780 in monthly revenue per unit. Combined, the two units generate $7,560 in monthly revenue. Operating expenses for these units, including cleaning, utilities, and management, total $2,400, resulting in net income of $5,160. The mid-term rental unit is leased for $2,200 per month, with minimal turnover and lower operating costs of $400 per month, resulting in net income of $1,800. The long-term rental unit is leased for $1,800 per month, with expenses of $300, resulting in net income of $1,500.

The total monthly income from the property is $11,560, with total operating expenses of $3,100. After accounting for the mortgage payment of $3,200, the net cash flow is $5,260 per month. This demonstrates the power of combining different rental strategies within a single property.

Over time, the investor optimizes the Airbnb units by increasing the average daily rate to $200 and improving occupancy to 75%. This increases monthly revenue per unit to $4,500, adding $1,440 in additional income across both units. The total property cash flow increases to $6,700 per month.

Additionally, the property appreciates to $660,000 over two years, creating $60,000 in additional equity. The investor performs a cash-out refinance, accessing a portion of this equity to fund the down payment for another multi-unit property. This allows the investor to replicate the strategy and scale the portfolio further.

This example illustrates how multi-unit properties and mixed rental models can significantly enhance both cash flow and scalability. By combining different income streams and optimizing performance, investors can create a highly efficient and resilient portfolio. The key takeaway is that multi-unit investing is not just about acquiring more units—it is about maximizing the potential of each property through strategic planning and execution.

Chapter 10

Advanced Airbnb Mortgage Structuring – Combining DSCR, Asset-Based, and Creative Financing to Close Any Deal

As investors reach the highest level of Airbnb portfolio building, the game is no longer about simply finding deals or qualifying for standard financing–it becomes about structuring deals in ways that allow you to close opportunities that others cannot. This is where advanced mortgage structuring comes into play. At this level, successful investors combine multiple financing strategies, layer different loan products, and creatively position themselves to overcome obstacles that would stop the average investor. This chapter focuses on how to structure complex Airbnb deals using DSCR loans, asset-based lending, and creative financing techniques to unlock unlimited growth potential.

The first shift in mindset at this level is understanding that there is almost always a way to structure a deal if the numbers make sense. Many investors walk away from opportunities because they do not fit traditional lending guidelines. Advanced investors, however, look at the deal from multiple angles and identify alternative ways to finance it. This may involve combining loan products, adjusting ownership structures, or bringing in additional capital sources. The goal is not just to qualify for loans, but to design financing solutions that align with the deal's potential.

DSCR loans remain a cornerstone of advanced Airbnb financing. These loans allow investors to qualify based on the income generated by the property rather than personal income. At scale, DSCR loans provide flexibility and speed, making them ideal for acquiring multiple properties. However, advanced structuring involves using DSCR loans strategically. For example, an investor may use a DSCR loan for one property while using a different financing method for another, optimizing the overall portfolio rather than treating each deal in isolation.

Asset-based lending introduces another powerful dimension to deal structuring. Instead of focusing on income, asset-based loans evaluate the borrower's liquid assets, such as cash, stocks, or retirement accounts. This allows high-net-worth investors or those with strong asset positions to qualify for loans even if their income is limited or complex. Asset-based lending can be particularly useful for bridging gaps in financing, allowing investors to secure properties while maintaining flexibility in their overall strategy. Creative financing techniques expand the possibilities even further.

These include seller financing, subject-to transactions, lease options, and private money lending. For example, seller financing allows the buyer to make payments directly to the seller instead of obtaining a traditional loan. This can be advantageous when dealing with motivated sellers or unique properties that may not qualify for conventional financing. Subject-to transactions involve taking over an existing mortgage, allowing investors to acquire properties with minimal upfront capital. These strategies require careful structuring and legal considerations but can provide significant advantages when used correctly.

Layering financing strategies is where advanced structuring truly shines. Instead of relying on a single loan product, investors can combine multiple sources of capital to complete a deal. For example, an investor might use a DSCR loan for the primary financing, supplement it with a private loan for the down payment, and negotiate seller concessions to reduce upfront costs. This layered approach allows investors to close deals that would otherwise be out of reach, while also preserving their own capital for future opportunities.

Cross-collateralization is another advanced technique used in portfolio structuring. This involves using multiple properties as collateral for a single loan, allowing investors to leverage existing equity to secure new financing. While this can increase borrowing capacity, it also ties properties together, meaning that issues with one property can affect the entire portfolio. As such, cross-collateralization must be used carefully and strategically.

Blanket loans offer a similar advantage by allowing investors to finance multiple properties under a single loan. This simplifies management and can provide access to larger amounts of capital. Blanket loans are particularly useful for investors with established portfolios who want to streamline their financing and reduce administrative complexity. However, they also require careful planning to ensure that the terms align with the investor's long-term strategy.

Another important aspect of advanced structuring is negotiating loan terms. Interest rates, loan duration, prepayment penalties, and reserve requirements can all be negotiated to some extent, especially when working with portfolio lenders or private lenders. Experienced investors understand that loan terms are not fixed and that negotiating favorable conditions can significantly impact cash flow and overall performance.

Deal structuring also involves optimizing ownership and entity structures. Holding properties in different entities can provide liability protection, tax advantages, and improved financing flexibility. For example, separating properties into different LLCs can reduce risk and make it easier to manage financing across the portfolio. Additionally, structuring ownership to include partners or investors can expand capital capacity and enable larger deals.

Another advanced concept is structuring deals with exit strategies in mind. Every acquisition should be evaluated not only for its immediate potential but also for how it fits into the long-term plan. This includes considering refinancing opportunities, potential appreciation, and resale value. By planning exits in advance, investors can ensure that each deal contributes to the overall strategy and provides flexibility for future decisions.

Speed and execution are critical at this level. In competitive markets, the ability to close deals quickly can provide a significant advantage. Investors who have established relationships with lenders, private investors, and partners can move faster and secure better opportunities. This requires preparation, organization, and a clear understanding of financing options.

Risk management remains essential when using advanced structuring techniques. While these strategies can unlock significant opportunities, they also introduce complexity and potential risks. Investors must carefully evaluate each deal, ensure that cash flow remains positive, and maintain adequate reserves. A disciplined approach to structuring ensures that growth is sustainable and aligned with long-term goals.

Ultimately, advanced mortgage structuring is about creating flexibility and opportunity. By combining multiple financing strategies and thinking creatively, investors can overcome limitations and continue to scale their Airbnb portfolios. This level of mastery allows investors to operate at a higher level, closing deals that others cannot and building a portfolio that grows beyond traditional constraints.

Real-Life Math Example: Structuring a Complex Airbnb Deal Using Multiple Financing Strategies

Consider an investor who identifies a high-performing Airbnb property priced at $800,000 in a prime vacation market. The property generates strong short-term rental income, with projected monthly revenue of $12,000 and operating expenses of $4,000, resulting in net operating income of $8,000. However, the investor does not have sufficient liquid capital to cover the full 25% down payment of $200,000 required for a DSCR loan.

To structure the deal, the investor uses a layered financing approach. First, they secure a DSCR loan covering 75% of the purchase price, resulting in a loan amount of $600,000. The monthly mortgage payment is approximately $4,200. This leaves a remaining $200,000 needed for the down payment and closing costs.

The investor then negotiates with a private lender to secure a second-position loan of $100,000 at an interest rate of 10%, with interest-only payments of $833 per month. This reduces the investor's required capital contribution to $100,000. To cover this remaining amount, the investor uses funds from a previous cash-out refinance and personal savings.

Additionally, the investor negotiates seller concessions of $20,000, which are applied toward closing costs. This reduces the total out-of-pocket investment to $80,000. By combining multiple financing sources, the investor is able to close the deal with significantly less capital than would be required under a traditional structure.

The total monthly expenses for the property include the DSCR loan payment of $4,200, the private loan payment of $833, and operating expenses of $4,000, resulting in total expenses of $9,033. With monthly revenue of $12,000, the net cash flow is $2,967 per month.

Over time, the investor optimizes the property, increasing revenue to $13,500 per month through improved pricing and occupancy. This increases net cash flow to $4,467 per month. After two years, the property appreciates to $900,000, creating $100,000 in additional equity.

The investor then refinances the property, paying off the private loan and securing a new DSCR loan at 75% loan-to-value, resulting in a loan amount of $675,000. After paying off the existing loans, the investor receives approximately $75,000 in cash, which is used to fund the next acquisition.

This example demonstrates how advanced structuring can enable investors to close deals with limited capital while maintaining strong cash flow. By combining DSCR financing, private lending, and seller concessions, the investor is able to acquire a high-performing property and create a pathway for future growth.

The key takeaway is that advanced mortgage structuring is not just about financing—it is about strategy. By understanding and combining different financing options, investors can unlock opportunities, accelerate growth, and build a portfolio that continues to expand without traditional limitations.

Chapter 11

Building Long-Term Wealth, Exit Strategies, and Legacy Through Airbnb Investing

As an Airbnb investor reaches the advanced stages of portfolio building, the focus begins to shift from rapid acquisition and scaling to long-term wealth creation, preservation, and strategic exit planning. While growing a portfolio is exciting and financially rewarding, true success is defined by how well that portfolio performs over time, how it supports your lifestyle, and how it can be leveraged to create generational wealth. This chapter explores how to transition from growth mode into long-term wealth strategy, including exit planning, portfolio optimization, and building a lasting financial legacy.

The first concept to understand is that wealth is not just measured by the number of properties owned or the amount of monthly cash flow generated—it is measured by control, flexibility, and sustainability. A portfolio that generates strong cash flow but is highly leveraged and unstable may not provide true financial security. Conversely, a well-balanced portfolio with manageable debt, consistent income, and appreciating assets can provide both stability and long-term growth. The goal is to build a portfolio that supports your financial independence while minimizing risk.

One of the most important aspects of long-term wealth strategy is portfolio optimization. As investors acquire properties over time, not all assets will perform equally. Some properties may outperform expectations, while others may underperform due to market conditions, location, or operational challenges. Periodically reviewing and optimizing the portfolio allows investors to identify opportunities for improvement. This may involve selling underperforming properties, reinvesting in higher-performing assets, or repositioning properties to increase revenue.

Exit strategies are a critical component of long-term planning. While the intention may be to hold properties indefinitely, having a clear exit plan provides flexibility and ensures that decisions align with long-term goals. Common exit strategies include selling individual properties, selling the entire portfolio, refinancing to extract equity, or transitioning properties into long-term rentals. Each strategy has its advantages and implications, and the choice depends on the investor's objectives, market conditions, and financial needs.

Selling properties can provide significant liquidity and allow investors to realize gains. For example, selling a property that has appreciated substantially can generate capital that can be reinvested into higher-performing opportunities or used to reduce debt. However, selling also involves transaction costs and potential tax implications, such as capital gains taxes. Investors must carefully evaluate whether selling aligns with their overall strategy and consider ways to minimize tax liabilities, such as using 1031 exchanges where applicable.

Refinancing remains a powerful tool even in the long-term phase of investing. By refinancing properties, investors can access equity, reduce interest rates, or adjust loan terms to improve cash flow. This can be particularly beneficial for stabilizing the portfolio and enhancing financial flexibility. Additionally, refinancing can be used to consolidate debt or restructure financing in a way that aligns with long-term goals.

Another important strategy is transitioning properties between rental models. As market conditions change, it may become advantageous to convert Airbnb properties into mid-term or long-term rentals. This can provide more stable income and reduce operational complexity, particularly for investors seeking a more passive approach. Conversely, properties can also be converted from long-term to short-term rentals to increase income potential. Flexibility in rental strategy allows investors to adapt to changing conditions and optimize performance. Debt management is a key factor in long-term wealth building. While leverage is essential for scaling, reducing debt over time can enhance stability and increase net worth. Investors may choose to pay down mortgages, refinance into lower-interest loans, or strategically eliminate high-cost debt. A balanced approach to debt ensures that the portfolio remains sustainable and resilient, particularly during economic downturns.

Tax strategy plays a significant role in preserving wealth. Real estate offers numerous tax advantages, including depreciation, deductions, and potential deferral of capital gains. Understanding and leveraging these benefits can significantly enhance overall returns. Working with tax professionals to develop a comprehensive strategy ensures that investors maximize their after-tax income and minimize liabilities.

Legacy building is the ultimate goal for many investors. This involves creating a portfolio that can be passed down to future generations, providing ongoing income and financial security. Structuring ownership through trusts or other legal entities can facilitate this process and provide additional benefits such as estate planning and asset protection. A well-planned legacy strategy ensures that the benefits of the portfolio extend beyond the investor's lifetime. Another important aspect of long-term strategy is lifestyle design. The purpose of building wealth is not just financial gain—it is to create the freedom to live life on your own terms. Investors must decide how actively they want to be involved in managing their portfolio and whether they prefer a hands-on or passive approach. This may involve transitioning to property management companies, reducing the number of properties, or focusing on high-performing assets that require less oversight.

Diversification beyond real estate can also enhance long-term wealth. While Airbnb properties provide strong income and appreciation, investing in other asset classes such as stocks, bonds, or businesses can provide additional stability and growth opportunities. A diversified portfolio reduces risk and ensures that wealth is not overly dependent on a single asset class.

Philanthropy and impact investing are additional considerations for investors seeking to create a meaningful legacy. By using their resources to support causes they care about, investors can make a positive impact while also benefiting from potential tax advantages. This adds another dimension to wealth, extending its value beyond financial metrics.

Continuous education and adaptation remain essential even at the highest levels of investing. Markets evolve, regulations change, and new opportunities emerge. Investors must stay informed and be willing to adjust their strategies to remain competitive and successful. This includes learning from experience, seeking expert advice, and staying engaged with industry trends.

Ultimately, building long-term wealth through Airbnb investing is about more than just acquiring properties—it is about creating a system that generates income, appreciates in value, and supports your desired lifestyle. By focusing on optimization, strategic exits, and legacy planning, investors can ensure that their portfolio continues to deliver value for years to come.

Real-Life Math Example: Transitioning a 12-Property Portfolio into Long-Term Wealth and Legacy

Consider an investor who has built a portfolio of 12 Airbnb properties over several years. Each property generates an average of $1,500 in monthly cash flow, resulting in total monthly income of $18,000. The combined value of the portfolio is $4.8 million, with an average loan-to-value ratio of 65%, resulting in $1.68 million in equity.

The investor begins by analyzing the performance of each property and identifies three underperforming assets generating only $800 in monthly cash flow each. By selling these properties at an average price of $350,000, the investor generates $1.05 million in proceeds. After paying off the remaining loan balances and transaction costs, the investor nets approximately $400,000 in cash.

This capital is reinvested into two higher-performing properties priced at $500,000 each, generating $2,000 in monthly cash flow per property. This increases total monthly income by $2,400, bringing the portfolio cash flow to $20,400 per month.

Next, the investor refinances four properties, reducing interest rates and extending loan terms. This decreases monthly mortgage payments by $300 per property, resulting in an additional $1,200 in monthly cash flow. The total portfolio cash flow now reaches $21,600 per month.

To reduce operational complexity, the investor converts four properties into mid-term rentals, reducing management costs by $200 per property. This adds $800 in monthly savings, increasing total cash flow to $22,400 per month.

The investor also allocates $200,000 into a diversified investment portfolio outside of real estate, generating an additional $1,000 in monthly passive income. This brings total monthly income to $23,400.

Over time, the investor continues to pay down debt and benefit from property appreciation. The portfolio value increases to $5.5 million, with equity growing to over $2.2 million. By maintaining strong cash flow and strategic management, the investor achieves both financial independence and long-term wealth growth.

Finally, the investor establishes a trust to transfer ownership of the portfolio to their family, ensuring that the assets continue to generate income for future generations. This creates a lasting legacy that extends beyond the investor's lifetime.

This example demonstrates how strategic optimization, refinancing, and diversification can transform a growing portfolio into a stable and sustainable source of long-term wealth. The key takeaway is that true success in Airbnb investing is not just about growth—it is about creating a system that endures, adapts, and provides value for generations to come.

Chapter 12

The Complete Airbnb Portfolio Blueprint — From First Property to Financial Freedom

At this stage of your journey, you have explored every major component required to build, scale, and optimize an Airbnb portfolio—from financing and deal structuring to operations, risk management, and long-term wealth strategies. Chapter 12 brings everything together into a complete, actionable blueprint that transforms knowledge into execution. This is where strategy becomes a system, and where your vision of financial freedom becomes a structured, repeatable process.

The first principle of the Airbnb portfolio blueprint is clarity of destination. Financial freedom means different things to different investors. For some, it may mean generating $5,000 per month in passive income to replace a job. For others, it may mean building a portfolio that produces $20,000 or more per month while continuing to grow in value. Defining your target income, timeline, and lifestyle goals is essential because it determines the size and structure of the portfolio you need to build. Without this clarity, it is easy to lose focus or pursue strategies that do not align with your objectives. The second principle is designing your portfolio backwards from your goal. Instead of randomly acquiring properties, you begin with your desired outcome and work backwards to determine how many properties are needed, what type of properties to acquire, and how they should perform. For example, if your goal is $15,000 per month in net cash flow and each property generates an average of $1,500, you would need approximately ten properties. This simple calculation provides a clear target and allows you to build a plan that is both realistic and measurable.

The third principle is phased growth. Scaling an Airbnb portfolio is not a single leap—it is a series of stages, each with its own focus and strategy. The first stage is acquisition, where the goal is to secure your first one to three properties and establish a foundation. The second stage is stabilization, where you optimize operations, improve performance, and build consistency. The third stage is scaling, where you leverage financing, systems, and equity to expand rapidly. The final stage is optimization and wealth preservation, where you refine the portfolio, reduce risk, and focus on long-term sustainability.

Financing strategy evolves across these phases. In the early stages, investors may rely on conventional loans or personal income to qualify. As the portfolio grows, DSCR loans, non-QM programs, and asset-based lending become more important. In advanced stages, investors combine multiple financing strategies, including equity recycling, partnerships, and portfolio lending. The blueprint emphasizes the importance of transitioning financing strategies at the right time to avoid bottlenecks and maintain growth momentum.

Deal selection is another critical component of the blueprint. Not every property is worth acquiring, and successful investors develop strict criteria for evaluating deals. This includes analyzing location, demand, property type, revenue potential, expenses, and financing terms. By maintaining discipline in deal selection, investors can ensure that each property contributes positively to the portfolio and aligns with their overall strategy. Over time, this consistency leads to a high-performing portfolio that is both profitable and scalable.

Operational systems are the backbone of the blueprint. Without efficient systems, scaling becomes difficult and unsustainable. This includes automation for guest communication, dynamic pricing tools, standardized cleaning and maintenance processes, and performance tracking systems. As the portfolio grows, these systems allow investors to manage more properties with less effort, improving both efficiency and profitability.

Cash flow optimization is integrated into every stage of the blueprint. From the first property to the final portfolio, investors must continuously analyze and improve performance. This includes adjusting pricing, increasing occupancy, reducing expenses, and optimizing financing. Small improvements at the property level compound significantly at the portfolio level, creating substantial increases in overall income.

Risk management is embedded throughout the blueprint. Diversification across markets and property types, maintaining adequate reserves, and monitoring regulatory changes are all essential for protecting the portfolio. The blueprint emphasizes a balanced approach to growth, ensuring that expansion does not come at the expense of stability. By managing risk proactively, investors can build a portfolio that withstands challenges and continues to perform over time.

Equity recycling and refinancing are key drivers of accelerated growth within the blueprint. By unlocking the value of existing properties and reinvesting it into new acquisitions, investors can create a compounding effect that speeds up portfolio expansion. This strategy reduces the need for new capital and allows investors to scale more efficiently.

The blueprint also incorporates advanced strategies such as multi-unit investing, mixed rental models, and creative financing. These approaches provide additional flexibility and opportunities for growth, allowing investors to adapt to different market conditions and maximize returns. By combining these strategies, investors can build a portfolio that is both diverse and resilient.

Performance tracking and data analysis are essential for continuous improvement. Investors must monitor key metrics such as revenue, occupancy, expenses, and cash flow across all properties. This data provides insights into what is working and what needs adjustment. By making data-driven decisions, investors can optimize performance and stay ahead of market trends.

Mindset and discipline are the intangible elements that hold the blueprint together. Building an Airbnb portfolio requires consistency, patience, and the ability to make informed decisions under uncertainty. Investors must remain focused on their long-term goals, avoid distractions, and continuously refine their strategy. The blueprint provides the structure, but execution depends on discipline and commitment.

Lifestyle integration is the final component of the blueprint. The purpose of building a portfolio is to create freedom and flexibility. Investors must design their systems and strategies in a way that supports their desired lifestyle, whether that means being hands-on or transitioning to a more passive role. By aligning the portfolio with personal goals, investors can achieve both financial success and quality of life. Ultimately, the Airbnb portfolio blueprint is a roadmap for transforming a single property into a scalable, income-producing system that generates long-term wealth. By following this structured approach, investors can move from uncertainty to clarity, from effort to efficiency, and from income to true financial freedom.

Real-Life Math Example: Building a Portfolio from 1 to 12 Properties Using the Complete Blueprint

Consider an investor who begins with a goal of generating $18,000 per month in net cash flow within five years. Based on an average of $1,500 per property, the investor determines that they need to acquire 12 properties to achieve this goal.

In year one, the investor acquires their first property for $300,000 with a 20% down payment of $60,000. The property generates $1,200 in monthly cash flow. Later in the year, they acquire a second property with similar performance, bringing total monthly income to $2,400.

In year two, the investor focuses on stabilization and optimization, increasing average cash flow per property to

$1,400 through pricing and operational improvements. They then acquire two additional properties using DSCR loans, bringing the total to four properties generating $5,600 per month. In year three, the investor leverages equity from the first two properties, performing a cash-out refinance that generates $80,000 in capital. This is used as down payments for two more properties, increasing the portfolio to six properties. Each property generates an average of $1,500 in monthly cash flow, resulting in total income of $9,000 per month.

In year four, the investor scales more aggressively by combining financing strategies and partnerships. They acquire four additional properties, bringing the total to ten properties. Through optimization and improved systems, average cash flow increases to $1,600 per property, resulting in total monthly income of $16,000.

In year five, the investor completes the portfolio by acquiring two final properties using accumulated cash flow and refinancing strategies. The portfolio now consists of 12 properties generating an average of $1,700 in monthly cash flow per property. Total monthly income reaches $20,400, exceeding the original goal.

Throughout this process, the investor maintains reserves, diversifies across markets, and continuously optimizes performance. Property values appreciate over time, increasing total portfolio value to over $4 million, with significant equity available for future opportunities.

This example demonstrates how a structured blueprint can guide an investor from their first property to a fully developed portfolio. By following a clear plan, leveraging financing strategies, and maintaining discipline, the investor is able to achieve financial freedom within a defined timeframe.

The key takeaway is that success in Airbnb investing is not accidental—it is the result of a well-designed system executed consistently over time. By applying the principles outlined in this blueprint, investors can build a portfolio that not only meets their financial goals but also provides lasting freedom and security.

Chapter 13

Mastering Consistency, Momentum, and Scaling Discipline

At the highest level of Airbnb investing, success is no longer determined by knowledge alone—it is determined by execution, consistency, and the ability to maintain momentum over long periods of time. Many investors learn the strategies, understand the numbers, and even acquire a few properties, but they fail to reach true financial freedom because they lack discipline and consistency. This chapter focuses on the final and most important layer of building an Airbnb portfolio: mastering the habits, systems, and mindset required to sustain growth and achieve long-term success.

Consistency is the engine that drives compounding results. In the early stages of investing, progress may feel slow, and results may seem modest. However, each property acquired, each system implemented, and each improvement made contributes to a larger system that grows over time. The key is to remain consistent in your actions, even when results are not immediately visible. Investors who stay committed to their strategy, continue acquiring properties, and continuously optimize their portfolio eventually reach a tipping point where growth accelerates and results compound rapidly.

Momentum is closely tied to consistency. Once an investor builds momentum, each action becomes easier and more efficient. Financing becomes smoother, deal flow increases, and operational systems become more refined. Momentum reduces friction and creates a positive feedback loop, where success leads to more opportunities. However, momentum can also be lost if consistency is broken. Long gaps between acquisitions, lack of follow-through, or inconsistent management can slow progress and make it difficult to regain traction.

One of the most important habits for maintaining momentum is setting clear, measurable goals. Investors should define both short-term and long-term targets, such as acquiring a certain number of properties per year or achieving a specific level of monthly cash flow. These goals provide direction and help maintain focus. Breaking larger goals into smaller, actionable steps makes them more achievable and allows for consistent progress.

Time management is another critical factor in sustaining growth. As the portfolio grows, the number of tasks and responsibilities increases. Without effective time management, investors can become overwhelmed and lose focus on high-value activities. Prioritizing tasks that directly contribute to growth—such as acquisitions, financing, and optimization—ensures that time is used efficiently. Delegating or automating lower-value tasks allows investors to focus on strategic decisions.

Decision-making discipline is essential for long-term success. Investors are constantly faced with opportunities, but not all opportunities are worth pursuing. Maintaining strict criteria for deal selection and avoiding impulsive decisions ensures that each acquisition aligns with the overall strategy. Discipline also involves knowing when to say no, even to deals that appear attractive on the surface but do not meet the required standards.

Another key aspect of consistency is maintaining financial discipline. This includes managing cash flow, maintaining reserves, and avoiding overleveraging. While aggressive growth can be tempting, it must be balanced with stability. Investors who prioritize financial discipline are better equipped to handle market fluctuations and unexpected challenges, ensuring that their portfolio remains sustainable over time.

Routine and structure play a significant role in maintaining consistency. Establishing daily, weekly, and monthly routines helps create a rhythm that supports productivity and progress. For example, investors may dedicate specific time each week to analyzing deals, reviewing performance metrics, or optimizing operations. These routines ensure that important tasks are consistently addressed and prevent critical areas from being overlooked.

Tracking progress is essential for maintaining motivation and accountability. By monitoring key metrics such as cash flow, property performance, and portfolio growth, investors can see the results of their efforts and identify areas for improvement. Tracking progress also provides a sense of accomplishment, reinforcing the importance of consistency and encouraging continued effort.

Adaptability is another important element of long-term success. While consistency is crucial, investors must also be willing to adjust their strategies in response to changing market conditions. This includes adapting to new regulations, shifts in demand, or changes in financing options. The ability to remain flexible while maintaining a consistent overall direction is what allows investors to navigate challenges and continue growing.

Mindset is the foundation of consistency and discipline. Building an Airbnb portfolio requires resilience, patience, and confidence. There will be setbacks, challenges, and periods of uncertainty, but maintaining a positive and focused mindset allows investors to overcome obstacles and continue moving forward. Viewing challenges as opportunities for growth rather than setbacks helps maintain momentum and reinforces long-term commitment.

Another important concept is compounding effort. Just as financial returns compound over time, so do the effects of consistent action. Each property acquired increases cash flow, which can be reinvested into additional properties. Each improvement in operations increases efficiency and profitability. Over time, these compounded efforts create exponential growth, transforming a small portfolio into a significant source of wealth.

Accountability is a powerful tool for maintaining discipline. Whether through mentors, partners, or personal tracking systems, having a mechanism for accountability ensures that commitments are followed through. This can include setting deadlines, tracking progress, or regularly reviewing goals. Accountability helps maintain focus and prevents procrastination or complacency.

Long-term vision ties everything together. While day-to-day actions are important, they must be aligned with a clear long-term goal. This vision provides motivation and direction, helping investors stay committed even during challenging periods. By keeping the end goal in mind, investors can maintain perspective and continue making decisions that support their overall strategy.

Ultimately, mastering consistency, momentum, and discipline is what transforms an investor from someone who owns a few properties into someone who builds a scalable, high-performing portfolio. These principles ensure that growth is not only achieved but sustained over time, leading to lasting financial success and freedom.

Consider an investor who commits to acquiring just two Airbnb properties per year over a five-year period. Each property generates an average of $1,200 in monthly cash flow. While this may seem modest at first, the power of consistency becomes evident over time.

Real-Life Math Example: The Power of Consistent Growth Over 5 Years

In year one, the investor acquires two properties, generating $2,400 in monthly cash flow. In year two, they acquire two more properties, bringing the total to four properties and $4,800 in monthly cash flow. By year three, the portfolio grows to six properties, generating $7,200 per month.

In year four, the investor acquires two additional properties, reaching eight properties and $9,600 in monthly cash flow. By year five, the portfolio consists of ten properties generating $12,000 per month. At this point, the investor has achieved a significant level of financial independence through consistent action alone.

However, the impact of consistency does not stop there. By optimizing operations and increasing average cash flow per property by $200 through pricing and efficiency improvements, total monthly income increases to $14,000. Additionally, property appreciation increases the overall portfolio value, creating equity that can be leveraged for further growth.

If the investor continues this pattern for another five years, acquiring two properties per year, the portfolio grows to 20 properties generating $28,000 per month. This demonstrates how consistent, disciplined action can lead to exponential growth over time.

The key insight from this example is that success does not require rapid or aggressive scaling—it requires consistent, focused effort over time. By committing to a clear plan and executing it consistently, investors can achieve significant results without taking on excessive risk.

This example highlights the importance of momentum. Each year builds on the previous one, creating a compounding effect that accelerates growth. The investor's experience, systems, and resources improve over time, making each subsequent acquisition easier and more efficient. Ultimately, the combination of consistency, discipline, and momentum creates a powerful pathway to financial freedom. By focusing on steady progress and long-term goals, investors can build a portfolio that grows predictably and sustainably, delivering lasting results.

Chapter 14

Creating Predictable Deal Flow and Building a Scalable Acquisition Machine

At the highest level of Airbnb investing, the difference between investors who plateau and those who continue scaling is simple: deal flow. You can have perfect financing, strong operations, and a clear strategy—but without consistent access to high-quality deals, growth slows down or stops entirely. The most successful investors do not rely on luck or occasional opportunities. They build systems that generate deals consistently, predictably, and at scale. This chapter focuses on how to create a deal flow engine that feeds your portfolio continuously and allows you to grow without limits.

The first mindset shift is moving from passive deal searching to active deal generation. Most investors browse listing platforms, wait for new properties to appear, and compete with dozens of other buyers. This reactive approach limits opportunities and often leads to overpaying. Advanced investors take control of their pipeline by creating multiple channels for deal flow. Instead of waiting for deals, they attract them. This is the foundation of building an acquisition machine. One of the most effective sources of deal flow is relationships. Real estate agents, wholesalers, brokers, and property owners are constantly exposed to opportunities. By building strong relationships with these individuals, investors can gain access to deals before they hit the market. Becoming known as a serious, reliable buyer is key. When agents know that you can close quickly and consistently, they are more likely to bring opportunities directly to you. Over time, this creates a steady stream of off-market deals that are not available to the general public.

Direct marketing is another powerful strategy for generating deal flow. This involves reaching out directly to property owners through methods such as mail campaigns, text messaging, or targeted advertising. By identifying properties that fit your criteria and contacting owners directly, you can uncover opportunities that others are not pursuing. This approach requires effort and consistency, but it can produce high-quality deals with less competition and more favorable terms.

Data-driven deal sourcing is becoming increasingly important in modern real estate investing. Tools and platforms that analyze market trends, rental performance, and property data can help investors identify high-potential opportunities quickly. By leveraging data, investors can focus their efforts on properties that meet specific criteria, improving efficiency and increasing the likelihood of success. This approach reduces guesswork and allows for more informed decision-making. Another key component of a scalable acquisition machine is having clear buy-box criteria. This is a defined set of parameters that every potential deal must meet. These criteria may include location, price range, expected cash flow, occupancy rates, and property type. Having a clear buy box allows investors to quickly evaluate deals and make decisions without overanalyzing. It also ensures consistency in acquisitions, which contributes to a more cohesive and high-performing portfolio.

Speed is a competitive advantage in deal acquisition. In many markets, the best deals are secured quickly, often before they are widely available. Investors who have their financing, systems, and decision-making processes in place can act faster than others. This includes having pre-approvals from lenders, access to capital, and a clear understanding of what constitutes a good deal. Speed not only increases the likelihood of securing deals but also strengthens relationships with agents and sellers.

Another important aspect of deal flow is conversion. Not every lead will turn into a deal, but having a structured process for evaluating and following up on opportunities increases conversion rates. This includes analyzing deals quickly, making competitive offers, and maintaining communication with sellers and agents. A strong follow-up system ensures that potential deals are not lost due to lack of attention or delayed responses. Scaling deal flow also involves building a team. As the number of leads increases, it becomes difficult for a single investor to manage everything. Hiring or partnering with acquisition specialists, analysts, or virtual assistants can help manage the pipeline and maintain efficiency. Each team member can focus on specific tasks, such as sourcing leads, analyzing deals, or coordinating transactions. This division of labor allows the acquisition machine to operate at a higher level.

Marketing your brand as an investor is another powerful tool for generating deal flow. By establishing a presence online, creating content, and positioning yourself as an expert, you can attract opportunities organically. Sellers and partners are more likely to approach investors who have a visible and credible brand. This can include social media, websites, or educational content that showcases your expertise and track record.

Consistency is the key to maintaining deal flow. Just like any system, the acquisition machine requires regular input and effort. This includes ongoing outreach, relationship building, and marketing. Even during periods when deals are being closed, it is important to continue feeding the pipeline to ensure future opportunities. Consistent effort leads to consistent results.

Another advanced strategy is stacking deal flow channels. Instead of relying on a single source, investors use multiple channels simultaneously. For example, combining agent relationships, direct marketing, and data-driven sourcing creates a diversified pipeline. This reduces reliance on any one source and increases overall deal volume. It also allows investors to adapt to changes in the market and maintain a steady flow of opportunities.

Financial preparation is essential for converting deal flow into actual acquisitions. Having access to capital, whether through personal funds, partnerships, or financing, ensures that opportunities can be acted upon quickly. Without financial readiness, even the best deals cannot be closed. This highlights the importance of aligning deal flow with financing strategies.

Tracking and optimizing the acquisition process is critical for long-term success. Investors should monitor metrics such as leads generated, deals analyzed, offers made, and deals closed. By analyzing these metrics, investors can identify areas for improvement and optimize their systems. This continuous refinement enhances efficiency and increases conversion rates over time.

Finally, mindset plays a crucial role in building a scalable acquisition machine. Investors must embrace persistence, adaptability, and a long-term perspective. Not every lead will result in a deal, and setbacks are inevitable. However, by maintaining focus and consistency, the acquisition machine will continue to produce results. Over time, this system becomes a powerful engine for growth, enabling investors to scale their portfolios predictably and sustainably.

Real-Life Math Example: Building a Deal Flow Machine That Produces 12 Properties in 2 Years

Consider an investor who sets a goal of acquiring 12 Airbnb properties within two years. To achieve this, they build a deal flow system that generates 50 leads per month from multiple sources, including agent relationships, direct marketing, and online platforms.

Out of these 50 leads, the investor analyzes approximately 30 properties in detail. Of those, 10 meet their buy-box criteria and are worth pursuing. The investor makes offers on these 10 properties each month. On average, 2 offers are accepted, resulting in 2 acquisitions per month during peak periods.

Over the course of a year, this system produces 12 acquisitions. Each property generates an average of $1,300 in monthly cash flow, resulting in $15,600 in monthly income by the end of the first year. In the second year, the investor refines their system, increasing lead generation to 60 leads per month and improving conversion rates. With improved efficiency, the investor now closes 1.5 deals per month on average, adding 18 properties over two years. However, due to capital constraints and strategic selection, they focus on acquiring the best 12 deals. These properties generate an average of $1,500 in monthly cash flow, resulting in $18,000 in monthly income.

The cost of running the deal flow system includes $2,000 per month for marketing and $3,000 per month for team support. Over two years, this totals $120,000 in expenses. However, the portfolio generates $18,000 per month in income, or $216,000 annually, more than offsetting the acquisition costs.

Additionally, property appreciation increases the total portfolio value to over $4 million, creating significant equity. This equity can be leveraged for further growth, compounding the results of the acquisition machine.

This example demonstrates how a structured deal flow system can produce consistent and scalable growth. By generating leads, analyzing deals, and maintaining a disciplined acquisition process, the investor is able to achieve their goal of building a 12-property portfolio within two years.

The key takeaway is that deal flow is not random—it is a system that can be built, optimized, and scaled. By creating a predictable pipeline of opportunities, investors can eliminate uncertainty and focus on execution. This transforms the process of acquiring properties from a challenge into a repeatable and controllable system, enabling long-term success and financial freedom.

Chapter 15

The Final Evolution — Turning Your Airbnb Portfolio into a Self-Sustaining Wealth Machine

At this stage, you are no longer simply an investor—you are the architect of a financial system that has the potential to operate independently of your time, grow continuously, and generate wealth for decades. The final evolution of Airbnb investing is not about acquiring more properties, optimizing a few numbers, or even scaling faster. It is about transforming your portfolio into a self-sustaining wealth machine—one that produces income, reinvests capital, adapts to change, and requires minimal active involvement from you. This is where true financial freedom is achieved.

The first principle of a self-sustaining portfolio is automation of income and reinvestment. In earlier stages, you actively worked to acquire properties, manage operations, and optimize performance. Now, the goal is to create a system where the income generated by your properties funds future growth automatically. This means establishing a process where a portion of your monthly cash flow is consistently allocated toward acquiring new assets, paying down debt, or investing in other opportunities. Over time, this reinvestment creates a compounding effect that accelerates wealth creation without requiring additional effort.

The second principle is operational independence. A portfolio cannot be considered a true wealth machine if it depends entirely on your daily involvement. Systems, teams, and automation must be in place to handle operations efficiently. This includes property management, guest communication, maintenance, and financial tracking. Whether through in-house teams or third-party providers, the goal is to ensure that the portfolio continues to function smoothly even if you step away. Operational independence allows you to shift your focus from managing properties to overseeing strategy.

Cash flow allocation becomes a strategic decision at this level. Instead of simply collecting income, you must decide how to deploy it effectively. This may involve reinvesting into new properties, paying down high-interest debt, building reserves, or diversifying into other asset classes. A structured allocation plan ensures that every dollar generated by the portfolio contributes to long-term growth and stability. For example, an investor may allocate 50% of cash flow to reinvestment, 30% to reserves and debt reduction, and 20% to personal income. Another key component of a self-sustaining portfolio is financial redundancy. This means creating multiple layers of income and protection within your portfolio. For example, having properties in different markets, using mixed rental models, and maintaining strong reserves all contribute to redundancy. If one property or market underperforms, the rest of the portfolio can continue to generate income. This reduces risk and ensures that the system remains stable under various conditions.

Debt strategy evolves in the final stage of investing. While leverage is essential for scaling, reducing debt over time can enhance stability and increase net worth. Investors may choose to pay down certain properties, refinance into lower-risk structures, or maintain a balanced mix of leveraged and unleveraged assets. The goal is to create a portfolio that generates strong cash flow while minimizing financial vulnerability.

Another important concept is portfolio optimization for efficiency. At this stage, investors may evaluate whether all properties are contributing effectively to the overall system. Underperforming assets can be sold or repositioned, while high-performing properties can be further optimized. This continuous refinement ensures that the portfolio remains efficient and aligned with long-term goals. Tax efficiency becomes increasingly important as income grows. Structuring the portfolio in a way that minimizes tax liabilities can significantly enhance net returns. This may involve leveraging depreciation, utilizing tax-advantaged entities, or planning strategic sales and reinvestments. Working with tax professionals ensures that the portfolio is structured for maximum efficiency.

Legacy planning is a defining element of a self-sustaining wealth machine. The portfolio is no longer just a source of income—it is an asset that can be passed down to future generations. Establishing trusts, estate plans, and ownership structures ensures that the portfolio continues to operate and generate income beyond your lifetime. This transforms your investments into a lasting legacy that benefits your family and future generations.

Another advanced strategy is creating additional layers of income beyond the properties themselves. This may include leveraging your experience to create educational content, consulting services, or partnerships. These additional income streams enhance the overall system and provide further diversification. They also allow you to monetize your knowledge and expand your impact.

Time freedom is the ultimate reward of building a self-sustaining portfolio. With systems and processes in place, you can choose how involved you want to be. Some investors continue to actively grow their portfolios, while others transition to a more passive role. The key is having the flexibility to make that choice. This freedom is what transforms financial success into a meaningful lifestyle.

Another important aspect of the final evolution is resilience. Markets will change, regulations will evolve, and unexpected challenges will arise. A self-sustaining portfolio is designed to adapt to these changes. This includes maintaining reserves, diversifying income streams, and continuously monitoring performance. Resilience ensures that the portfolio not only survives challenges but continues to thrive.

Compounding remains the driving force behind long-term wealth. As income is reinvested and properties appreciate, the portfolio grows exponentially. Each cycle of reinvestment increases the base from which future growth occurs. Over time, this compounding effect can lead to significant wealth, far beyond what is possible through linear growth.

Mindset at this stage shifts from growth to stewardship. You are no longer just building wealth—you are managing and preserving it. This requires a long-term perspective, disciplined decision-making, and a focus on sustainability. By adopting this mindset, you ensure that your portfolio continues to deliver value for years to come.

Ultimately, the transformation into a self-sustaining wealth machine is the culmination of everything you have learned. It is the point where your portfolio operates as a system, generating income, reinvesting capital, and adapting to change. This is the true definition of financial freedom—a system that works for you, rather than one that depends on you.

Real-Life Math Example: Turning a 15-Property Portfolio into a Self-Sustaining Wealth Machine

Consider an investor who has built a portfolio of 15 Airbnb properties, each generating an average of $1,500 in monthly cash flow. This results in total monthly income of $22,500, or $270,000 annually. The investor's goal is to transform this portfolio into a self-sustaining system that continues to grow without requiring additional personal capital.

The investor begins by allocating 50% of monthly cash flow, or $11,250, toward reinvestment. This capital is used to acquire one new property every six months, with each property requiring $70,000 in total investment. Over two years, this results in the acquisition of four additional properties, bringing the total to 19 properties.

Each new property generates $1,400 in monthly cash flow, adding $5,600 to the portfolio. The total monthly income increases to $28,100. At the same time, the investor allocates 30% of cash flow, or $6,750 per month, toward reserves and debt reduction. Over two years, this results in $162,000 in reserves and significant reduction in loan balances.

The remaining 20% of cash flow, or $4,500 per month, is used for personal income, providing financial freedom while maintaining growth. As the portfolio grows, appreciation increases the total property value from $5 million to $6.2 million, creating additional equity.

The investor then optimizes operations, increasing average cash flow per property by $200 through pricing and efficiency improvements. With 19 properties, this adds $3,800 in monthly income, bringing the total to $31,900 per month.

By reinvesting income, reducing debt, and optimizing performance, the portfolio becomes increasingly self-sustaining. New acquisitions are funded by existing income, and the system continues to grow without requiring additional external capital.

Over a five-year period, the portfolio expands to 25 properties, generating over $40,000 in monthly cash flow. At this point, the investor has achieved a level of financial independence where the portfolio not only supports their lifestyle but continues to grow automatically. This example illustrates the power of compounding and reinvestment. By creating a system where income fuels growth, the investor transforms their portfolio into a self-sustaining wealth machine. The key takeaway is that true financial freedom is achieved when your investments generate enough income to support both your lifestyle and future growth.

At this level, the portfolio is no longer just a collection of properties—it is a dynamic system that evolves, adapts, and expands over time. By applying the principles outlined in this chapter, investors can achieve the ultimate goal of Airbnb investing: a self-sustaining, scalable, and enduring source of wealth.

Final Thoughts

As you reach the end of this journey through the Airbnb Mortgage Loan Mastery Series, it is important to pause and recognize how far you have come—not just in knowledge, but in perspective. What may have started as curiosity about short-term rentals or a desire to earn extra income has now evolved into a complete system for building, scaling, and sustaining wealth through Airbnb investing. You are no longer thinking like a beginner. You are thinking like a strategist, a builder, and ultimately, an owner of a financial system that has the potential to change your life and the lives of those around you.

Throughout this series, you have learned that success in Airbnb investing is not about luck, timing, or even finding the "perfect" deal. It is about understanding the process, applying consistent strategies, and building a system that works over time. From your first property to a fully scaled portfolio, every stage has its own challenges and opportunities. But with the right knowledge and approach, each stage becomes a stepping stone rather than a barrier.

One of the most important lessons is that financing is not a limitation—it is a tool. Early on, many investors believe that lack of income, capital, or experience will prevent them from moving forward. However, as you have seen, there are multiple financing strategies available, including DSCR loans, non-QM programs, asset-based lending, and creative financing techniques. The key is not to fit into a single box, but to understand how to use these tools strategically to achieve your goals. When you begin to see financing as flexible rather than restrictive, new opportunities open up.

You have also learned that scaling is not about doing more—it is about doing better. Acquiring more properties without systems, strategy, and discipline leads to chaos. But building a portfolio with intention, structure, and efficiency creates momentum and long-term success. Each property should serve a purpose within your portfolio, contributing to your overall goals and strengthening your financial position. This shift from random growth to strategic scaling is what separates average investors from those who build true wealth.

Another critical takeaway is the power of systems and automation. At the beginning, managing one property may feel manageable, even simple. But as your portfolio grows, complexity increases. Without systems, that complexity becomes overwhelming. With systems, it becomes manageable and even scalable. Automation, delegation, and standardization allow you to operate at a higher level, freeing up your time to focus on growth and strategy. This is the transition from working in your business to working on your business.

Risk management is a theme that runs through every stage of this journey. While Airbnb investing offers significant income potential, it also comes with uncertainties. Market fluctuations, regulatory changes, and operational challenges are all part of the landscape. The goal is not to eliminate risk, but to manage it intelligently. Diversification, reserves, and strategic planning provide the stability needed to navigate challenges and continue growing. A well-structured portfolio is not just profitable—it is resilient.

As you progressed through the series, you began to see how each component connects to the others. Financing supports acquisitions. Acquisitions feed the portfolio. Operations sustain performance. Optimization increases profitability. Refinancing unlocks equity. And equity fuels further growth. This interconnected system is what transforms individual properties into a scalable wealth machine. When each part is aligned and functioning properly, the entire system becomes greater than the sum of its parts.

You have also explored advanced strategies that elevate your investing to the next level. Multi-unit properties, mixed rental models, creative financing, and deal flow systems all provide additional pathways for growth. These strategies are not necessary in the beginning, but they become essential as you scale. They allow you to overcome limitations, access new opportunities, and continue expanding your portfolio even in competitive markets.

Perhaps one of the most powerful concepts you have learned is the idea of compounding. Just as interest compounds in a savings account, your efforts, investments, and systems compound over time. Each property adds to your income. Each improvement increases your efficiency. Each decision builds on the previous one. Over time, these compounded effects create exponential growth. What starts as a single property can evolve into a portfolio that generates substantial income and wealth.

But beyond the numbers, there is a deeper purpose to this journey. Financial freedom is not just about income—it is about choice. It is about having the ability to decide how you spend your time, where you focus your energy, and what kind of life you want to live. For some, this means leaving a traditional job. For others, it means having the flexibility to travel, spend time with family, or pursue personal passions. Your Airbnb portfolio is not just a financial asset—it is a tool for creating the life you envision.

Legacy is another important dimension of this journey. As your portfolio grows, it becomes more than just a source of income—it becomes an asset that can be passed down to future generations. By structuring your investments thoughtfully and planning for the long term, you can create a lasting impact that extends beyond your lifetime. This transforms your efforts into something meaningful and enduring, providing opportunities and security for those who come after you.

It is also important to recognize that this journey is ongoing. The real estate market will continue to evolve. New technologies will emerge. Regulations will change. The strategies that work today may need to be adapted in the future. Continuous learning and adaptability are essential for long-term success. By staying informed, remaining flexible, and continuously refining your approach, you can navigate these changes and continue to thrive.

Discipline and consistency remain the foundation of everything you have learned. No strategy, no system, and no opportunity will produce results without execution. The most successful investors are not necessarily the most talented or the most experienced—they are the most consistent. They show up, they take action, and they follow through. By committing to consistent effort over time, you create momentum that carries you forward even when challenges arise.

As you move forward, remember that every step matters. Your first property matters. Your second property matters. Each decision, each improvement, and each action contributes to your overall progress. There is no need to rush or compare yourself to others. Focus on your plan, your goals, and your journey. Progress, no matter how small, is still progress.

You now have the knowledge, the strategies, and the framework to build something truly powerful. The question is no longer whether it is possible—it is whether you are willing to take action. The opportunities are there. The tools are available. The path has been outlined. What remains is execution.

Your Airbnb portfolio has the potential to become more than just an investment—it can become a system that generates income, builds wealth, and creates freedom. It can support your lifestyle, provide for your family, and leave a lasting legacy. But like any system, it requires effort, attention, and commitment.

As you close this chapter and move into the next phase of your journey, carry with you the understanding that you are in control. You have the ability to design your future, to build your portfolio, and to create the life you want. The process may not always be easy, but it is always worth it.

This is not the end—it is the beginning of what comes next.

How to Get a Personalized Airbnb Mortgage Loan Review

If you found this book helpful, you may want to see how these strategies apply to your own financial situation and investment goals. Every investor's profile is unique. Property type, location, projected Airbnb income, credit score, available capital, and lending guidelines all impact what loan programs you may qualify for and how your deal can be structured.

The examples in this book are designed to teach how Airbnb mortgage loans work—but your real options can only be determined by reviewing your specific numbers and investment scenario.

You can request a no-obligation Airbnb mortgage loan consultation here:

Email: info@FinibiMortgage.com

A licensed mortgage professional will review your scenario and explain what Airbnb financing options may be available to you, including DSCR loans, Non-QM programs, and alternative qualification strategies based on your property and financial profile.

No cost. No pressure. No obligation.

Sincerely,

Joseph G. Correa

Licensed Mortgage Loan Originator

Finibi Mortgage Inc.

About the Author

Joseph G. Correa is a licensed mortgage broker and the founder of Finibi Mortgage, a Florida-based brokerage specializing in real estate investment financing, Airbnb and short-term rental loans, and alternative lending strategies for investors, entrepreneurs, and self-employed borrowers. With more than two decades of experience in mortgage lending, underwriting, and financial structuring, Joseph has helped thousands of clients secure funding using intelligent, flexible loan strategies designed for modern real estate investing.

Unlike traditional loan officers who focus only on closing transactions, Joseph's approach is rooted in long-term wealth building. He believes that mortgage financing—especially for Airbnb and investment properties—should be used as a strategic tool to generate cash flow, scale portfolios, and create financial independence. His philosophy centers on using leverage intelligently, allowing investors to grow without relying solely on personal income or traditional lending limitations.

Joseph is widely recognized for his expertise in DSCR loans, Non-QM lending, short-term rental financing, bank statement programs, and creative deal structuring. He specializes in helping investors qualify based on property income rather than personal income, making it possible for beginners, self-employed individuals, and experienced investors to acquire and scale Airbnb portfolios. His ability to simplify complex lending concepts into clear, actionable strategies has empowered countless individuals to enter the real estate market with confidence.

Joseph created *The Airbnb Mortgage Loan Mastery Series* to give investors the same financing knowledge used by banks, private lenders, and institutional real estate operators. His mission is simple: to help people understand how to qualify, structure deals, and scale using modern lending strategies—so they can build profitable Airbnb businesses and long-term wealth.

When he is not structuring deals or writing, Joseph works directly with investors and borrowers across the United States to design customized financing strategies that align with their goals, property types, and growth plans.

The Airbnb Mortgage Loan Mastery Series Roadmap

The Professional Guide to Financing, Scaling, and Profiting from Short-Term Rental Properties

The purpose of *The Airbnb Mortgage Loan Mastery Series* is to give investors the same financing strategies used by banks, lenders, and institutional real estate operators—translated into clear, practical guidance for everyday investors. Each book builds on the last, taking you from foundational knowledge to advanced deal structuring, portfolio scaling, and long-term wealth creation using Airbnb and short-term rental properties.

Book 1 — Airbnb Mortgage Loan Fundamentals This book gives you the foundation. You will understand how Airbnb mortgage loans work, what makes them different from traditional financing, and how lenders evaluate short-term rental properties. You will learn the core concepts of DSCR, Non-QM loans, and income-based qualification, along with who qualifies and how to structure your first deal. Every book that follows builds on this knowledge and shows you how to apply it to real-world investing.

Book 2 — DSCR Airbnb Mortgage Loans This book focuses on one of the most powerful tools in Airbnb investing: DSCR loans. You will learn how to qualify using rental income instead of personal income, how DSCR is calculated using short-term rental data, and how to position your property to meet lender requirements. This book shows you how to break free from traditional income limitations and scale faster.

Book 3 – Airbnb Mortgage Loans for Beginners This book is designed for first-time investors. You will learn how to buy your first Airbnb property using the right loan strategy, how to analyze deals, and how to overcome common obstacles. It provides a clear, step-by-step path from zero experience to your first successful investment.

Book 4 – Airbnb Investment Property Mortgage Loans This book focuses on scaling. You will learn how to finance multiple Airbnb properties, build a portfolio, and optimize cash flow. It introduces strategies for acquiring properties efficiently and managing them as part of a larger system.

Book 5 – Airbnb Mortgage Loans with No Income Verification

This book explores advanced qualification strategies. You will learn how to get approved without tax returns using DSCR, bank statement, and alternative documentation programs. It is designed for self-employed borrowers and investors who want flexibility in how they qualify.

Book 6 — Luxury Airbnb Mortgage Loans
This book focuses on high-end properties. You will learn how to finance luxury Airbnb investments, analyze high average daily rates, and balance risk with return. It introduces jumbo loan strategies and premium market positioning.

Book 7 — Airbnb Mortgage Loans for Vacation Homes
This book explains how to finance second homes and convert them into profitable short-term rentals. You will learn the difference between second home and investment property guidelines, along with hybrid usage strategies and compliance considerations.

Book 8 — Airbnb Mortgage Loan Refinancing & Cash-Out Strategies
This book teaches you how to unlock equity and scale faster. You will learn how to refinance Airbnb properties, execute cash-out strategies, and recycle capital into new investments.

Book 9 — Airbnb Mortgage Loans for Multi-Unit Properties
This book focuses on duplexes, triplexes, and small multifamily properties. You will learn how to finance multiple income streams within one property, analyze mixed rental models, and navigate zoning and compliance.

Book 10 — Advanced Airbnb Mortgage Loan Structuring

This book brings everything together. You will learn how to combine DSCR, asset-based, and creative financing strategies to close complex deals. It is designed for investors who want to operate at a high level and scale without limits.

This series is designed to be followed step by step or used as a reference based on your current stage. Whether you are just starting or already building a portfolio, each book provides the tools, strategies, and insights needed to move forward with clarity and confidence.

The goal is simple: to help you understand how to finance, structure, and scale Airbnb investments so you can build a profitable, long-term real estate business.

Educational & Financial Disclaimer

This book is provided for educational and informational purposes only. The author and publisher are not engaged in rendering legal, tax, accounting, investment, or financial advice. Although Joseph G. Correa is a licensed mortgage loan originator, the information in this book is intended to provide general education about Airbnb mortgage loans, DSCR financing, and short-term rental investment strategies—not personalized financial, legal, or lending advice.

Mortgage programs, underwriting guidelines, interest rates, credit requirements, and short-term rental financing options vary by lender, investor, state, and economic conditions, and may change at any time without notice. The examples, calculations, and scenarios presented in this book are hypothetical and are for illustration purposes only. They do not represent guaranteed results, loan approvals, or actual investment outcomes.

Short-term rental performance, including Airbnb income, occupancy rates, and average daily rates, is influenced by market demand, competition, seasonality, management quality, and local regulations. These factors can vary significantly and are not guaranteed. Before making any financial decisions—including purchasing an Airbnb property, applying for a DSCR or Non-QM loan, refinancing, or using real estate financing for investment purposes—readers should consult with a qualified mortgage professional, financial advisor, tax advisor, or attorney who can evaluate their specific situation.

Risk Disclosure

Real estate investing and short-term rental financing involve risk. Airbnb properties rely on variable income, which can fluctuate due to changes in demand, competition, economic conditions, and local regulations. There is no guarantee that a property will achieve projected income levels or maintain consistent occupancy.

Borrowing to purchase or refinance investment properties increases financial leverage and risk. Failure to make required mortgage payments could result in foreclosure or loss of property. DSCR and Non-QM loans may carry higher interest rates, stricter terms, or prepayment penalties, which can impact long-term profitability.

Additionally, changes in laws or regulations governing short-term rentals may affect your ability to operate a property as an Airbnb. Investors are responsible for ensuring compliance with all local, state, and federal regulations.

This book teaches structured, strategic, and responsible approaches to Airbnb financing and investing, but no strategy is risk-free. Readers are solely responsible for their financial decisions and outcomes. Neither the author nor the publisher makes any warranties, express or implied, regarding the accuracy, completeness, or applicability of the information in this book to any individual situation.

www.ingramcontent.com/pod-product-compliance
Lightning Source LLC
LaVergne TN
LVHW022223200926
848481LV00006B/2097
9798295801228